'Class Peace'
An Analysis of Social Status and English Cricket 1846-1962

Eric Midwinter

First published in Great Britain by
Association of Cricket Statisticians and Historians
Cardiff CF11 9XR.
© ACS, 2017

British Library Cataloguing-in-Publication Data.
A catalogue record for this book is available from the British Library.

ISBN: 978 1 908165 86 2
Typeset and printed by The City Press Leeds Ltd

Contents

Introduction

This is the first volume in a new series called *'Cricket Witness'* which explores through primary and secondary sources a number of themes in cricket history. Over the course of the coming years, it is hoped that further volumes will be produced covering contemporary topics and recent history, in addition to themes from the 18th and 19th centuries.

We are delighted that Eric Midwinter, an eminent cricket historian and former senior officer of the Association should launch the series with a typically erudite and scholarly analysis of a pivotal theme in cricket history.

I would be delighted to hear from other authors who would like to contribute to what we hope will be a major series by the Association, and building on the excellent reputation of the *'Lives in Cricket'* series. Anyone who wishes to contribute should contact me in writing at the Association's address or by email to higgers2015@outlook.com

Andrew Hignell
Hon. Secretary ACS
and Series Editor

Prologue

In 1849 began the serialisation of Charles Dickens' *David Copperfield*. Like Dickens before him at the behest of his father John Dickens, the eponymous hero was forced as a ten year old to work for a time in a blacking factory. He was horrified, finding this much more shocking than his ill-treatment at, literally, the hands of his stern step-father Edward Murdstone or his cruel teacher Mr Creakle. The commentator Arthur Calder-Marshal, writing of Dickens' similar distrait experience, aged eleven, asserted that one cannot understand the depth of this feeling 'unless one realises the social barrier at that time between the artisan class...and the educated class to which John Dickens belonged. The artisan had to remain in that 'state to which God had called him': the educated could rise (as Charles Dickens did rapidly later) to the social heights.'[1]

David Copperfield took flight, sought out his great-aunt Betsy Trotwood in Dover and overnight was restored to the rank of young gentleman, schooled under the gentle rein of the scholarly Dr Strong. Charles Dickens, too, had been released from his brief conscription into the artisan ranks, moving on to Wellington House Academy, Mornington Place, London, an establishment which, although somewhat in the Creakle tradition, rendered him once more one of the 'educated class'. Yet he never forgot but rarely mentioned this agonising subject, apart from seeking catharsis through writing David Copperfield. In particular, he remained pained throughout his life that his mother Elizabeth Dickens had been, as he termed it, 'warm' for him to continue working in the blacking factory. The six shillings he earned weekly were of inestimable value for one whose husband was impecunious and debt-laden – but, such was the then social mind-set, John Dickens suffered little stigma from being cast in Marshalsea debtors' prison, while his son was temporarily branded contemptible lower class for sticking labels on blacking bottles alongside 'common boys.'

It was in that kind of social atmosphere that cricket, having reached something of a nadir in the Regency years and thereafter, was in the ascendant, heading inexorably towards being a comprehensively national sport and entertainment. Like all other enterprises and institutions, it had to come to terms with the prevailing class system. It did so by formalising the nascent practice of distinguishing fairly rigidly as between the gentry or those who aspired thereto and the paid players and other cricketing help-meets such as groundsmen who were all indubitably artisan in styling. As a gentleman you could potter in your own garden and/or pay for a gardener – but you couldn't be seen doing someone else's garden for money. The same with cricket. If help was hired, it was from a tradesman, not a 'professional', using that ambiguous word in its later 'white collar' sense. However, as with much else in that society, stratagems were found for 'educated' and 'artisan' participants to play or watch together.

Fortunately, there had been precedents in the Georgian epoch when forms of cricket were induced in London and the south-east into something of an identifiable format under the pressure of heavy gambling. The patrons of those matches were not averse from recruiting, initially through their own employees, paid help from the lower classes. For a brief spell cross-class teams were fielded – and the notion of the paid player had stamped itself sufficiently on the game for it to survive. It did so, much strengthened, when cricket re-emerged in improved moral guise after the collapse of the gambling craze.

The class-related phenomenon of 'Gentlemen and Players' was soon accepted as the normal descriptor. It is often viewed, according to political taste, as a wholesome jolly of cavalier toffs and cheery rustics or a grim exploitation of abject proles by arrogant gaffers. The association of social class and English cricket is, of course, much more nuanced than that. In particular, the period 1846 to 1962, book-ended in cricketing terms by the first outings of William Clarke's 'Exhibition' XI and the end of the purported amateur/professional distinction, also approximates to the era in which the concept of social class impinges most forcefully on the English psyche.

Cricket, most compellingly at county and international but also at club and school levels, has much to tell about the incidence of social class consciousness and practice during this period – just as an understanding of this same class dichotomy in society in general throws light on cricket's class issues.

In overall terms, the period under major review was a hundred years or so marked by a counter-intuitive harmony as between earnest middle class and aspiring working classes. This was forged against a background of state-sponsored improved conditions, for which the most apt technical term is Collectivism. This embraced local as well as central government not least in those activities ascribed as 'rational recreation' by Victorian authorities. Hundreds of cricket matches played in municipal parks is a model example of this tendency.

With shared values and interests, the two classes, making up over 80% of the population, prompted a kind of voluntary alliance, best described as 'cultural integration'. There was much shared in common, although the spheres of that sharing were clearly marked – for instance, the train with its 'class' compartments. Thus the sight of three Victorian or early 20th century amateurs emerging from one dressing room and through one gate and eight professionals from another room and through another gate to find common ground in a joint enterprise is the perfect microcosm, arithmetically correct, of social conditions from mid-19th to mid-20th century.

Moreover, if less regulated, something of the same was to be found in certain elements of recreational cricket while, more significantly, spectatorship of the first-class game was similarly patterned. One is able to trace something of a two-tier, loosely class-based attendance at such matches during the same period. This exemplifies a feature of this era; the relatively peaceful crowd, the crowd that was not feared. This was at variance with the 150 years before the 1850s when the crowd was rightly held in some dread. One might further argue that beyond the 1960s, at the other end of the period under review the crowd came again, with association football the prime example, to be regarded with apprehension.

From 1846 to 1962 it was, on the whole, 'class peace' rather than class war – but with no relaxation of the class distinction *per se*.

This study seeks to analyse and illustrate this vital piece of cricket history by fitting the cricket piece as neatly as is feasible into the complex jig-saw of society during this hundred year era. It reached from primary post-industrial times to the middle of the 20th century.

Since then the mood and the conditions have shifted once more from a more collectivist and co-operative to a more neo-liberal and individualistic age, in many ways more 18th than 19th century in character. The social and cultural coalition that had endured for a hundred years disintegrated. Once more cricket illustrated the switch. When first-class performers were all deemed to be 'Cricketers', they became, formally, by all the yardsticks used in such analysis, 'Gentlemen', that is, middle class. Some of this same proclivity was to be seen in the recreational game. Importantly, cricket's audience also followed suit, with spectators largely middle class and, in part by that token, in penny numbers except on rare occasions such as Test matches. Ironically, the collapse of first-class cricket as a regular crowd-drawer may have saved it from some of the problems faced by the football authorities. Whether the novel attraction of the Twenty20 format will affect this comparative quietude or, like the previous one-day schedules, enjoy but temporary popularity is another question for another day.

It is that pre-1962 age, dominated by some fluid alignment of the working and middle classes, which provides the canvas for this picture of English cricket in its most mature and penetrative epoch. The two classes were so near...and yet so far. Charles Dickens and 'his favourite child David' Copperfield contrived to switch relatively simply from one class to the other and back again. W.G.Grace, born a few months before David Copperfield, could not afford economically to be a 'gentleman' nor socially to be a 'player', so, as Cassius said of Julius Caesar, he 'doth bestride the narrow world like a Colossus', with a Shamateur foot in either camp.

---

1   A.Calder-Marshal in his 'Introduction' to David Copperfield Pan Classic 1967.

Chapter One

Pre-Victorian Society; 'Gentle And Simple'

Pantomime, like cricket, has a lengthy tradition of lore mixed with controversial roots. By the middle of the 19th century, just as cricket was preparing to present itself in modern clothing as a leading wholesome national spectator sport, pantomime, too, was cast in updated healthy form. Its ancient Harlequinade formation was gradually morphing from up to 400 titles to just a few standard plots still familiar today. Joe Grimaldi had introduced the 'dame' character in 1812 and by the 1870s this had become firmly established along with the four former Harlequinade staples. Using *Jack and the Beanstalk* as an example, the five main cast were and often remain Mistress Trott, Jack, the Princess, the King and, as old-fashioned 'Clown' – Simple Simon.[1]

Over time 'Simple' has acquired the connotation of dimness. Instinctively, many people believe that when confronted by the wily pieman, he was not the brighter of the pair, even if he does eventually prevail. For Simple Simon – whose nursery rhyme dates from 1764 - was plebeian rather than foolish. Simple was the descriptor of the lower orders in those years gone by; the upper orders were 'gentle'. Both terms, obviously if confusingly, have a number of meanings attached, with 'simple' running a gamut from uncomplicated to stupid, but, during the 18th century and until in the following century when the class construct took hold, they offered the main social reference points. While 'simpleman', unlike simpleton, never took hold, 'gentlemen' did in a most emphatic way, enduring as a social indicator well into the 20th century.

An account of how cricket developed during these years, especially in London and its environs, into a public entertainment linked with sometimes heavy gambling, is, one trusts, instructive. It might help with an understanding of how, when cricket burgeoned into a mainstream national recreation and spectator sport in Victorian times, there was a rather unusual and timely accommodation of the knotty class question. Some useful precedents had been created.

In the pre-industrial age the coupling of terms gentle and simple was a constant, with 'gentlemen' liberally used for cricket teams from those early days. Gentle folk and simple folk were also common terms. In a letter dated as late as 1852, the great sage Thomas Carlyle, writing to his friend Arthur Helpe, talks of 'Scotch (sic) gentlefolk and simple-folk', although the use of the hyphen in the second suggests it was not so commonplace as the first term. Carl Wells, commenting on Gwendoline Keats/Zack's historical novel *Life is Life* (1898) says that the authoress 'understood that gentle folk and simple-folk are both people. Humphrey is a young gentleman and Wilkie is of a class far below him, but Wilkie easily holds his own as a person of both intelligence and dignity, in their conversation. At the same time there is no denial that class differences exist.'

The seminal Grand National of 1839, backed by many (but not all, for horse racing like cricket, is not free from historical controversy) as the first of that name, attracted a crowd probably over-estimated of 50,000. It was composed of the gentry and the nobility who had danced and dined in the nearby stately homes for a week beforehand and who were prepared to pay the extravagant price of 7s (35p but something like £40 or £50 in modern value) to watch and wager on the race.. They were joined by 'piemen, chimney sweeps, cigar sellers, thimble-riggers and all the small fry of gaming-table keepers' among a swarm of ordinary mortals; the *Liverpool Courier* added 'our inns have been crowded with gentle and simple.'[2]

As a reminder that cricket was not alone in developing cross-class sport, this was the first of these major Aintree steeplechases which was not exclusively open to 'gentlemen'. Nine gentlemen riders were joined by eight professional jockeys. For the record, Jem Mason on 'Lottery' won the race, Captain Becher on 'Conrad having set off 'at a spanking pace', only to take a tumble at the ditch that thereafter bore his name.

As a final example, *The Ingoldsby Legends* which the eloquent R.H.Barham began publishing in 1837 include the stanza from *The Hand of Glory; the Nurse's Story*

> Gentle and simple, squire and groom
> Each one has sought his favourite room

These instances of the 'gentle'/'simple' usage are deliberately chosen to show how common it was until deep into the 19th century. Such divisions depend largely on people accepting the nomenclature. Everyone, like it or not, knew where they stood in the social order, although there were, of course, many delicately framed gradations in both ranks. Moreover, the prevailing moral and religious code, as is perhaps the wont of such creeds throughout history, justified these drawn lines of the social gulf in no uncertain terms. From at least the time of ancient Egypt, institutionalised belief sought to uphold the *status quo* of the established social system. Bang on cue for the start of the period under main review, it was in 1848 that Cecil Frances Alexander published her charming Anglican hymn, *All Things Bright and Beautiful* with its imperishable verse of how God made them high and lowly - and *ordered* their estate, with the unsung corollary that there is no point struggling against divine ordinance.

For all that, these were never caste systems. Two famed Thomases – Wolsey and Cromwell, respectively the sons of a butcher and a blacksmith – rose to and fell from great heights, while a third Thomas, Becket of that ilk, was but the son of a textile trader. With gifts, grit and good fortune it was just possible to make occasional forays across the social frontier. They were so occasional as to give rise - as all three of those famed Thomases discovered - to sardonic comment among their contemporaries who refused to believe that blood was thinner than the fresh water of talent. They were sufficient, nevertheless, to give a wisp of encouragement to aspiring 'grooms' and, perhaps more importantly, a straw of comfort to the 'squires' that theirs was not a tyrannically closed community.

More significantly from the stance of this analysis, it accorded some leeway for inter-class activity, such as eight professional and nine amateur riders contesting a horse race on equal terms. The precedent provided by Hanoverian and Regency cricket in this regard whilst by no mean a technical model for the future was, at best, the bestowal of a blessing that it was possible for men from separate social levels to play or watch cricket together under some form of special dispensation.

Having established the premiss, how did 'gentle' and 'simple' come together cricket-wise in the 18th and early 19th century? The brief answer is with difficulty and not frequently. However, this had more to do with social environment than with social classification. Some grasp of this difficulty is necessary to comprehend how the reverse social circumstances of the later period were so much more contributive to cricket played and watched nationally and across the class divide.

Chroniclers of the history of particular games have mostly attempted to trace the lineage of their chosen diversion backwards, optimistically seeking an origin, doubtless anxious to add the lustre of antiquity to their favoured sport. Except for games played exclusively by the top brass, the conditions of Georgian and Williamite Britain were not conducive to the development of all-inclusive national sporting pastimes. The original game of tennis came to be called 'real' that is as in royal, tennis by journalists early in the 20th century when the new-fangled lawn variety was becoming exceedingly popular. Real tennis was one of those exceptions that prove the rule that before the industrial revolution sport was rough and ready and extremely diverse. The only fully recognised games were very expensive and very synthetic.

Tennis itself had taken some three centuries to evolve around and for the nobility of France, picking up a racket along the way where once a glove had been deployed. Its elaborate gallery of a court derived from monastic and abbey cloisters where primitive versions had been played and, by 1600, Paris alone housed 250 of these venues, strictly for royalty and noble families. Shakespeare shows his usual grasp of upper class vernacular when Henry V, insulted by the Dauphin's sneering gift of tennis balls, cries that he will 'play a set shall strike his father's crown into the hazard...all the courts of France will be disturbed with chases', set, hazard, court and chase being tennis terms. Henry VIII, as probably Shakespeare was aware, had built a tennis court at Hampton Court in 1530. Anne Boleyn, it is reported, was leisurely watching some former-day Andy Murray when she was arrested. In the 17th century there were fourteen courts in London and the sport boasts the longest running world championship, as from 1760. Expensive, architecturally complex, stylised rules, as carefully guarded as per participants as a knightly tourney, it was not a pastime you could run out and have the Tudor equivalent of a kick about for an hour or so in the

Tudor equivalent of your back garden.[3]

Because that, in the main, was what, for the multitude of the population, outdoor activities - a few youths perhaps knocking a ball about for a brief spell - amounted to until well into the 19th century. Several factors were at work that ensured this. The first of these was the atomised nature of community life. England and Wales was constituted of no less than 15.000 parishes and, outside of the few large towns, these were relatively isolated and indeed some of them were quite widespread themselves as to housing. The population of the UK, after a period of decline, had struggled to 7m in 1731 and grown to 9m in 1801, the beginnings of the major demographic leap allied with the industrial revolution. Outside the relatively few good-sized towns, most of those 15,000 parishes, with 300 inhabitants some kind of rough average, housed scarcely enough in most cases for any serious sporting development. Even by the accession of Queen Victoria in 1837, over half of the work-force were still devoted directly to agriculture or to its associated activities and mostly living in small village communities.

Even as late as the 1880s, as Flora Thompson reveals in her pastoral reminiscence, it was eight miles from Lark Rise to Candleford and a matter of excitement among neighbours, when Laura aka Flora went to work in the post office there. 'Come the summer, we'll...all go over to Candleford, their father said for the ten millionth time. Although he had said it so often they had never been. They had not been anywhere farther than the market town for the Saturday shopping.' That was three miles away. Oxford, the nearest city, was a distant nineteen miles, XIX on a milestone no more than a magical sign of some legendary and mysterious land.[4]

This, of course, was a vestige of a dying past but it demonstrates how secluded, over a hundred years after the industrial era had first began to stir, most of life was. Back in the 18th century with farming the chief occupation, the labouring population was tied to the agrarian economy socially as well as financially. The vast majority of people had not the time, nor the money nor perhaps the inclination to reach outside their families and neighbours for what snatches of opportunity they had for recreation.

As late as 1830 the average number of public transport journeys undertaken annually was only four per head. This amounted to 75m trips. On a normal weekday just 220,000 such journeys were undertaken, no less than 95,000 of them in London. The remainder was made up of 20,000 on longer distance coach rides, 20,000 on minor, provincial road services and, perhaps, surprisingly, 85,000 on the newly developed steamboats.[5] And this was all a vast improvement brought about by some betterment in the roads system from the dreadful potholes and other impediments of most of the 18th century. There were at least some 'flying' coaches, and maybe some wagon or carrier services, on the trunk roads, some 'short-stage' coaches and a few horse-drawn buses in the big towns, as well as coastal and river steam-boats. Before the advent of the Turnpike Trusts and the Macadamised roads, water transport had been very important. It had often been easier to travel by river and sea from London to Brighton than by road. It used to take a longer time to get from London to York than to Calais. Improved roads, for instance, had reduced the travel time from London to Manchester to one day. During the 18th century it had taken three days. The canal network, although not making much of a contribution to passenger transit, had led to a reduction of 75% in freight costs. Canals were ponderously slow. It took twelve hours by canal from Manchester to Liverpool.

G.M.Trevelyan wrote of the 'unremedied badness of the roads', legally the responsibility of the parishes through which they passed. The parochial authorities had neither the resources nor the ambition to do much about these route ways. When the weather was inclement, especially in the winter months, wheeled traffic came to a complete standstill. Josiah Wedgwood's renowned Etruria pottery, built in the 1770s, had pack-mules to convey his attractive wares for the first part of their carriage to customers and he reckoned that a third were broken on that leg of their journey because of the rough terrain.

It was not an entirely immobilised society – but it was a pedestrianised one. Few had access to a horse for personal conveyance. That was a perquisite of the wealthy. Even then the daily radius for a journey by horse was little more than fifteen miles. It was, basically, a nation of walkers. Even in London 90% of journeys under six miles were on foot. Jane Eyre and *Tess of the D'Urbevilles* in fiction and Charles Dickens and William Gladstone in fact bear testimony to that. What is often not factored in with regard to recreational history is the time-consuming nature of walking. Gladstone thought nothing of walking home to Hawarden from Chester station having travelled from London. It is an eight mile hike and it took him a couple of hours, exactly the current rail journey time from London to Chester.

When William Pitt the Younger decreed in 1803 that all able-bodied men must join the militia, a version of the home guard, against the peril of Napoleonic invasion (although his sceptical critics would argue that this was part of 'Project Fear', deploying the French menace to distract from domestic strife and misery) he advised there should be two weekly parades. However, he added that these should not be more than six miles from anyone's home, 'no more', he said 'than the sturdy English peasantry were in the habit of going when led to a cricket match or other rural diversion.' Twelve miles walking was not in itself an improbable exercise but, after arriving home after a hard day in the fields and having attended, as many perforce had to do, to one's domestic plots, the notion of spending another five or six hours walking and parading was out of the question. Numerically, the scheme was a success but it is thought most of the militia parades remained quite local and in the more heavily populated townships. Being 'led' to a cricket match was an interesting usage by William Pitt. It does indicate the sense of a special occasion, some holiday or festive event rather than a regular occurrence.

The combine of lengthy working hours and inadequate transport facilities told against more than a modicum of movement for all but a few rare and doubtless prized occasions. In 1846, the starting-point of the central component of this study, Charles Pearson, a journalist and commentator, asserted that the English were 'chained to the spot'.

Indeed they were for the most part chained to the spot legally as well as socially by the settlement laws. Vigorous attempts were made to restrict the ceaseless movement that so much alarmed the authorities. The settlement laws obliged all those in houses of less than £10 annual rental – often the yardstick for the 'simple' and 'gentle' division and also one of the devices used for electoral eligibility- to return to and/or remain in their parish. This was because one's home parish had the responsibility, were one a vagrant or pauper, to provide poor law aid. No ratepayer wanted to be forking out money for other people's misfits. It was today's complaints about immigrants scrounging off national benefits writ small. In general, it was a not terribly efficient way of trying to prevent the lower classes roaming all over the place.

For the period before about 1840 was a restless one, characterised by dislocation and stress. From the onset of the Industrial Revolution until today, with cricket frequently used as a picturesque illustration, many have mourned the loss of the rural idyll. There is more than a note of romantic fancy in this pastoral fallacy. Whatever the coming hardships of industrial experience, few migrants to the factory town regretted their move. For example, a study based on the memoirs and journals of 350 such industrial incomers found no longing for agrarian bliss.[6] Starvation wages, the problem of finding winter work, the oft forgotten nastiness of rural child labour and a general fear of exploitation had been the norm.

What still existed of the common ownership of land was all but obliterated by the Agricultural Revolution, particularly in the later part of the 18th century and in the decades up until the General Enclosure Act of 1845. It was tantamount to an industrial approach to farming, involving pastoral and arable agriculture alike over much more extensive areas. Commons and smallholdings were 'inclosed' by purchase or more substantially by parliamentary legislation. In the hundred years up to 1850 a third of the farmed land, some 14m acres, was thereby enclosed in a torrent of legislation, leaving 200 persons owning half the nation's land. One incidental side-effect was the takeover of land used for common-or-garden recreation.

But the human consequences were much more severe than merely lost 'play' opportunities. A landless host was created. Thousands, losing their own land tenures and the rights to common land, either became agricultural labourers or migrated to the towns. It is sometimes said, perhaps at some risk of simplification, that the enclosure movement recruited the industrial proletariat. This massive destabilisation of the rural economy and the beginnings of modern urban growth coupled to produce a restlessness of very unsettling proportions. It contributed to the very high level of disorder, what has been called a 'flourishing economy of crime', that disrupted society.[7]

In the chaotic atmosphere of the times, there was much petty theft and minor lawlessness, as a mass of people who had been driven from the land, drifted hither and thither, moving randomly about seeking for odd jobs or, perhaps more positively, trying to migrate into the merging industrial townships. In great alarm and with no police force of any effectiveness, the authorities reacted in a draconian fashion. The military were often called out and there were, on average, 115 executions every year.

'Oligarchy moderated by riot' is how one contemporary wag defined the Hanoverian era and its aftermath.. There was constant disorder. It was close to class war as the populace faced up to the government and the local squirearchy time after time. The frequent elections – there were ten in twenty years during one phase – were normally marked by violence and drunkenness at the open air meetings and public casting of votes. Charles Dickens' *The Pickwick Papers*, published 1836/37 but set some twenty or years earlier, includes a comical sketch of the Eatanswill election – 'Fizkin's people have got three and thirty voters in the lock-up coach house at the White Hart' . Dickens had covered such contests as a copy journalist and his description has a realistic tone. There were innumerable 'bread riots' when prices were forced up by poor harvests, higher demand as population grew and the continuing protection against foreign imports of corn. There were as many as 200 bread riots in the decades from 1720 to the opening of the next century.

The continuous economic woes were the cause of much trouble. In 1765 the Spitalfields Riots saw silk workers lay siege to Bedford House, the Duke of that ilk being a supporter of the importation of French silks. Come the application of new machinery with, suspected or genuine, the laying off of workers and there were outbreaks of desperate violence. The machine breaking campaign that came to be known as Luddism lasted intermittently between 1811and 1817; the riot so vividly described in Charlotte Bronte's 1849 novel *Shirley* is set in this period. There was the 1817 March of the Blanketeers when Lancashire weavers attempted to walk to London to protest against harsh trading conditions, carrying a blanket as both an emblem of their trade and for nightly comfort. Troops, regular and local yeomanry or militia, were often used to put down such adventures, often with extreme violence. As a result of the 'Captain Swing' arson attacks on agricultural goods and equipment in 1830-32, 600 were imprisoned, 500 were transported and 29 were executed.

There was unrest of a more political causation. The John Wilkes 'Liberty' riots of 1768 and thereafter, which included the incident in 1771 when a small knot of his supporters were killed by troops in the 'Massacre of St George's Fields' is one such, while the Gordon Riots of 1780 in London is another. Fuelled by anti-Roman Catholic hysteria, the tale and the story of the baying crowd, burning and damaging Newgate prison and the homes of London 'Papists' is told in terrifying detail in Charles Dickens' *Barnaby Rudge*. It is unsurprising that the Riot Act, which allowed magistrates to call for the disbandment of an assembly of twelve or more people, was an 18th century statute passed in 1714.

In the wake of the French Revolution of 1789 radical opinion was both buoyed by its adherents and suspected by its opponents. Among several disturbances, there were the Spa Fields Riots of 1816, followed by the episode of the Cato Street Conspiracy in 1820, a desperate attempt to assassinate the prime minister and cabinet. With rumours of the employment of government spies and *agents provocateurs*, it was a messy business all round.

The culmination of this unrest was the Peterloo Massacre of 1819, so called in mockery of the great victory at Waterloo a few years earlier. A crowd of 60/80,000 had gathered on St Peter's Fields, Manchester, chiefly to listen to speeches favouring the reform of parliament but, as so often, against a background of social discontent. The authorities commanded cavalry and local yeomanry to disperse the crowd. Although, given the panic and chaos, numbers have a degree of uncertainty, around fifteen were killed and between 400 and 700 injured. Lord Liverpool's government's response was the swift passage of the 'Six Acts', each of them retaliatory and suppressive of movement, speech and publication.

During a period when Britain was frequently at war there were further hazards, such as the costly burden of hostilities disrupting some elements of trade or demobilised soldiers and naval 'press gang' recruitment adding to anxieties. The militia and yeomanry which politicians like William Pitt the Younger sought to enlist, did most of their fighting at home, Peterloo being one instance. There was also actual warfare on the home front. Apart from two Irish Rebellions in 1798 and 1803, both put down by military means, there were the more famous Jacobite Rebellions of 1715 and 1745.

The Jacobite Rebellions, attempts to reinstate the Stuart dynasty, were serious affairs. Both were suppressed by strong military action. In particular, the Battle of Culloden in 1746, the very last pitched battle to be fought on British soil, was a merciless and bloody affair. In consequence there followed the 'Highland Clearances', aimed at breaking up the clan system and also driven by the landowners' wish to switch from small-scale agrarian units to large areas devoted to sheep-grazing and deer-stalking. The clearances were the equivalent of the English enclosures. They were intensified in the Regency era and accompanied by often brutal evictions, sometimes as many as 2000 such incidents in a day.

In brief, neither the social environment of the age nor the character of its people was propitious for the evolution of a formalised, nationally accepted field sport of any kind.

1.   Gyles Brandreth Discovering Pantomime (1973) for a detailed description of these changes.
2.   Eric Midwinter 'The First Grand National' ch.2 pp. 40-52 Old Liverpool (1972).
3.   Max Robertson Encyclopaedia of Tennis (1974).
4.   Flora Thompson *Lark Rise to Candleford* (originally in three separate volumes; first joint publication 1945).
5.   Jack Simmons *The Victorian Railway* (1991) for this reference but also as the definitive study of transport during the rest of the 19th century when public transport played so enormous a role in the furtherance of cricket along with all major sports.
6.   Emma Griffin *Liberty's Dawn; A People's History of the Industrial Revolution* (2013).
7.   Paul Langford *A Polite and Commercial People; England 1727 to 1783* (1992) for this reference but also as a general survey of the era. This is a slightly tongue-in-cheek title as Professor Langford reveals the full 'Hogarthian vulgarity' of the times.

Chapter Two
Pre-Victorian Society And Sport

Under the veneer of Georgian grandeur of architecture, arts and fashion, the country was more a heaving mass of often impoverished despair, simmering with lawlessness and violence. The authorities' attitude to games playing was antagonistic. This was no new-found enmity. From early in the 14th century onwards there is a lengthy roster of royal proclamations and edicts prohibiting the playing of games by the lower orders. For example, in 1541 a statute of Henry VIII's reign forbade the playing of games, the prohibition expressly listing artificers, labourers, apprentices and servants. The law allowed games only at Christmas and then only under the beady eye of one's master and at his home. That decree was not repealed until 1845, just at the beginning of cricket's epoch of success, although, of course, the 1541 and subsequent similar legislation had long been largely ignored.

Such efforts at social control were motivated by both political and economic arguments. In 1555 Queen Mary I legislated against sports because they might be used as a screen by 'treasonable Protestants' to conspire against her Popish rule. In the 1650s the Puritan ban on games during Oliver Cromwell's Protectorate was in part influenced by anxieties that renegade Royalists might similarly be plotting a Stuart restoration. The playing and watching of games was also judged to be a distraction from honest toil. In 1793 the *Gentleman's Magazine* was alarmed by the gathering of people for leisure purposes which 'propagates a spirit of idleness at a juncture when, with most industry, our debts, taxes and decay of trade will scarcely allow us to get our daily bread'.

The religious gloss on social control was also featured in the Hanoverian approach. Compared with and possibly as a reaction against the acrimony of religious conflict in the 16th and 17th centuries, the 18th century church was lax and complacent, with the nation's theological energy sapped. Indeed, 'enthusiasm' was now frowned upon in terms of religious profession. Henry Fielding's Reverend Mr Thwackum in his novel *The History of Tom Jones* (1749) Jane Austen's Reverend William Collins in *Pride and Prejudice* and *Emma's* Reverend Philip Elton are splendidly comic examples of Anglican pomposity and lassitude at that time. In so far as they were active, the clergy generally backed the local squirearchy in the protection of its rights. The denial of outdoor leisure opportunities was shrouded in moralistic proscriptions in regard of the wickedness of idleness. Sanctions against playing games on the Sabbath, the only free day for most people, was the crux of this tactic.

As is so often the case where there is a cyclic confrontation of stern governance and fractious governed, the resultant violence and misbehaviour appeared to justify the strong line taken by the alarmed authorities. Predictably, this aggression was as endemic in sport as in general conduct. Football involved large and motley bands, fighting and struggling for hours. There was bull-baiting and cock-fighting and there was bare-fisted pugilism that lacked any hint of control. Even the primitive forerunners of cricket that were played included, in some versions, charging and the use of the bat to interfere with fielders. Many of the early references to cricket allude to injuries and court cases. Unruly hosts were drawn to such events, most of them associated with or sponsored by taverns, keen to sell their alcoholic beverages to often belligerent crowds.

All in all, the prevailing circumstances told against any national or fundamental development of regular or regulated sport. Two historians from differing generations and mind-sets might be quoted. G.M.Trevelyan, of the old school, had this to say:

'When we try to imagine how the generality of our ancestors disported themselves out of doors, we must remember that most of them lived widely scattered and in the country. For most men the village was the largest unit of their intercourse. A village cricket match, or hurly-burly at football, or races on the green was very different from the 'organised athletics' of the modern arena. But most people took their 'exercise' as a matter of course in doing their work, in tilling the fields, or on walking or riding in and from their daily task...

Few villagers had seen anything of town-life... No city-made newspapers or magazines stamped a uniform mentality on the nation. In this isolation from the world at large, each shire, each hamlet had its own traditions, interests and character...For gossip and sensation they were satisfied with the daily human drama of their own village.'[1]

Writing of these same detached, closeted and tiny leisure activities and representing a more modern echelon of historians, Robert Malcolmson, the leading scholar of the popular pastimes of this time, concluded from his deep study of the subject that 'it is likely that these routine leisure activities and family festivities were, in terms of the hours involved, more prominent than the large public celebrations and sporting events'. What he terms 'informal face-to-face encounters' constituted the bulk of Georgian recreation.[2]

One may readily gather how cut off from mainstream flows was the majority of the pre-industrial population - indeed, it might be claimed that there were few mainstream flows. Pleasures, when available, were taken domestically and locally, singly or in small numbers. Folk-games and activities were in the cultural ascendant. Later social commentators would talk in darkened whispers of the anomie of industrial city life, but there was also considerable isolation in rural life with families and knots of people left very much to their own limited devices.

One must admire and respect the chroniclers of pre-industrial cricket.[3] They have dredged through countless primary sources to uncover whatever scrap of reference to cricket might be found. The exhausting hours spent on this research has been commendable and it is safe to aver that we have a record of most cricket played before, say, 1840. It does not add up to much. The arduous prospecting should act as a warning that the occasional glints of gold in the muddy dross are rare and the hope of striking it rich is a vain one. How the cricket historian might envy, say, the criminologist researching 18th century law and order; there the testimony is huge and overwhelming.

The secluded and separated playing of games that so dominated the 18th and early 19th century sporting landscape has led to a further error in interpretation. Like an old fire-horse pricking its ears at the sound of the bell, the mention of 'cricket' in a newspapers or court return immediately throws up for the cricket addict the image of a recognisable cricket match. Unluckily, and certainly until well into the 18th century, there is really no detailed description of what the players were actually doing.

There may have been hundreds of varying types of cricket, just as there may well have been scores of other cricketing games which were called something else. To the modern mind, concentrated on the feature of fixtures and conformity to an agreed formula, such kaleidoscopic variety seems unreal. A year or so ago the question was raised in the press of 'if Blackheath were the first rugby club, who did they play against?' Allowing for the truth of the premiss raised, the simple answer is 'one another'. Rather like the golf or badminton club today, these were groups of people playing for an hour so among themselves. Except on special occasions and very limited in regional incidence, there was no need for a grand design of rules. It was no one else's concern but that of the immediate group at play – and if they changed their rules the following evening, that was strictly their business. Flora Thompson again, remembering that she was writing of a time toward the end of the 19th not the 18th century: 'A few of the youths and younger men played cricket in the summer. One young man was considered a good bowler and he would sometimes get up a team to play one of the neighbouring villages.' As late as that and a game was still an occasional rather than a regular occurrence on some parts of the Northants-Oxfordshire border.

Once the historian attunes him or herself to this pivotal truth, much of the rest of pre-modern cricket history falls into place. If cricket deserves to be included in the silver treasures of civilisation, then it follows that it might be newly interpreted by the same recent and advanced theories about the origins of agriculture, writing and the like. Modern studies assert that, rather than emulation and imitation of a single root, there has been spontaneous combustion, with human groups autonomously discovering or developing these basic civilising devices.[4] Similarly with 'play', what Johan Huizinga, the Dutch cultural theorist, happily defined as the essential 'interlude' or respite from work and other heavy responsibility, which has evolved seamlessly in all human groupings.[5]

Hence it is unnecessary, even wasteful, to attempt to trace modern sports, such as football or cricket or hockey, back to some birthright, even if cricket-lovers, like all devotees of a religious cult, have yearned to seek out cricket's Bethlehem or Mecca, for religions, of course, are a case-study themselves in spontaneous uprising. Bethlehem and Mecca are as shrouded in myth as Harry Altham's shepherds on the Weald (those shepherds have a habit of turning up at the nativity of religions) or Rowland Bowen's controversial Irish or Flemish first-ever cricketers.[6]

By far the most accomplished gold miners, seeking for originating nuggets, are Peter Wynne-Thomas, with his carefully reasoned critique of previous false claims and his geographically pursued course to the iron workers of the Sussex Weald, and John Eddowes, whose brilliant linguistic studies demonstrate how Flemish weavers brought cricket to Kent. Both know that the author admires them with equal deference and that he judges them both to be right. Cricket, like all games that have not been artificially invented like basketball (1891, James Naismith) or the snooker variation (1875, Neville Chamberlain – no, not that one...) have multiple origins.[7]

Just to take a couple of instances of the mixture of 18th century play, Prince Frederick Louis, eldest son of George II and heir to the throne, a cricket enthusiast and inveterate gambler, is said to have died in 1751 from being hit with a cricket ball, Horace Walpole, youngest son of the Sir Robert Walpole, has been pooh-poohed and dismissed as games-slacker and aesthete for confusing it with a tennis ball, although, at that time, it is possible the same ball could have used for both purposes. It may have caused an abscess which later burst but the prince also caught a chill, which turned to pleurisy, while supervising his gardeners at Kew on a cold March day, hardly cricket weather. He died on 20 March with general medical opinion now opining the actual cause of death was pneumonia.[8]

Equally confusing is Samuel Johnson's definition of cricket in his famous dictionary, published in 1755, as a game 'in which the contenders drive the ball with sticks in opposition to each other', suggestive of a brisk exercise in hockey. Harry Altham, writing almost 200 years later in 1926 and unable to contemplate his beloved cricket being played in so sprightly a fashion, judged this to be a 'less happy' error. It would be intriguing to arrange an ethereal confrontation of the two and eavesdrop on the grand lexicographer's riposte. It is not beyond the bounds of speculation that Samuel Johnson had witnessed, say, a band of London apprentices diverting themselves as he described and calling it 'cricket'.

Once one accepts the Darwinian rather than the Creationist explanation, the evidence in which cricket is entwined with so many other games is the more explicable. Peter Wynne-Thomas properly points out that cricket must be a late developer because it has so many elements overtly borrowed from other groups of games, including bowling (as in bowls, skittles *et al.*), hitting (as in baseball, rounders, hockey *et al.*) and running (as in athletics, the football codes *et al.*) One might add the rather strange defence of two targets rather than in one, as in football, rugby and hockey, not forgetting the charging allowed in early forms of the game. There are plenty of examples of how cricket has been thus influenced by some of the other genres but the chief point is the lateness of its coming to maturity.

Thus the genuine historical question is not where did cricket start but when and how did cricket emerge from the morass of 'gameness' as a discrete sport, nationally recognised and nationally regulated.

It is at this point that the 'simple' and 'gentle' equation also manifests itself. It is only when the latter take up the cricketing cudgels with some degree of sharing with the former that a prescriptive typology of cricket appears. It is generally agreed that the principal if not the exclusive factor in this development was gambling.

The canvas to this was the gradual shift of mercantile life from a more straightforward matter of trading with a relatively uncluttered handling, buying and selling of goods to a new dimension of large scale investment and complex fiscal instruments – the Bank of England, for example, was established in 1694 and gradually became the key agency – involving both government and private operators. Since the Glorious Revolution of 1688/89 and the consolidation of parliamentary sovereignty, finance had become more standardised. Monarchs for years had had to take out commercial loans and levy taxes to meet their bills with subsequent pressure to 'redress grievances' as part of the bargain. Now this was government business. For example, the crippling cost of the War of the Spanish Succession (1701-14) was £150m against a normal peacetime government expenditure of only £2m annually. Parliament had to assume responsibility for loans, with its credit-worthiness reliant on the understanding that the propertied and moneyed classes would ensure that debts were paid. It meant that much rested on the collaboration of the governing regime and the rich. It was an oligarchy. It was a plutocracy.

Hereby was constructed a financial apparatus that was somehow detached from the trading arm of the economy. It signalled the rise of the financial sector. Much of previous commerce had engaged merchants in direct business transactions, including loans, in goods and products with which they were familiar. Now through the medium of stocks and shares a financial market developed alongside the actual workaday economy. The imperial element supported this, with both the Indian sub-continent and the West Indies at the forefront. The South Sea Bubble which burst in 1720 was the classic and foremost illustration of the frenzy of fiscal speculation that was in evidence at this time. It was, in a word, gambling.

Gambling was the major Georgian vice. The success especially of overseas trade in the second half of the 17th century had filled the coffers of the upper classes. Apart from mercantile speculation, huge amounts were laid on wagers on all kinds of hazards. Had some of the Puritan grandees who had striven to enrich their families by arduous graft been able to witness how their descendants wasted their hard-won assets, they would have been shocked. An oversimplification of the line-up for the English Civil War tends to place the nobility wholly on the royalist side but the Duke of Bedford and the Earl of Warwick were but the leading two peers central to the Parliamentary cause. With their fortunes based on overseas trade, they were mightily suspicious of the caprice of monarchical government.[9]

The mania for gambling in stocks and shares proved infectious. Cards, especially, but also lotteries, were the key indoor games, with horse racing, pugilism, cricket and 'pedestrianism', that is, running races, the principle outdoor pursuits that attracted the gamblers. The lower orders joined in where they could, with crown and anchor and pitch and toss as well as cock-fighting and bear-baiting their more specific preserve. The esteemed 18th century historian J.H.Plumb asserted that gambling was a national palliative against the unstable, disorderly and grisly conditions of the time. It was, he concluded 'an antidote favoured by all classes.'[10]

The manner in which the Hanoverian nobility and gentry adopted cricket has been finely analysed by David Underdown in clear and persuasive detail.[11]

At first sight, a 'simple' knockabout diversion of inconsistent format does not seem readily appropriate for the 'gentle', as opposed, for instance, to the mixed economy of riders in a horse race, for the upper echelons of society were well used to riding hard after hounds. The advantage the cricket typology had over some of the rougher pastimes was, however, that, with charging and hitting the ball twice, with the risk of injury to others, soon shunned, the physical contact which may have been demeaning was limited, At the same time, this was a manly, open-air sport. Gentlemen were keen to demonstrate to their peers and underlings alike that they were not effete. Cricket was a noble compromise.

The boys of the gentry were wont to play with the boys of the labourers on the big farms and estates, something of which is illustrated by the semi-autobiographical story of Tom Brown, published in 1857. His progenitor Thomas Hughes was born in 1822 in Berkshire and was at Rugby from 1834 to 1842, just at the dawn of modern cricket. It should not be forgotten that the first three chapters deal with Tom's dealings and exploits with the village lads. That juvenile interface with the lower orders must have immensely aided the development of cross-class cricket teams.[12]

But the wager was often the primary motive. It followed that the construct of the game had to be exactly understood so that the betting could be fairly resolved. It is no accident that the first testimony we have of a formal regulo for cricket is a written concordat for such a match – according to John Arlott, a match involved gambling, a game didn't. It dates from 1727. It is the 'Articles of Agreement' for two fixtures between teams raised by the 2nd Duke of Richmond and Mr Alan Brodrick. For those fearful that a mere commoner might have been overwhelmed by the occasion, it should be added that Alan Brodrick succeeded to the title of Viscount Midleton in 1729. The Articles are described as 'instructions' for the avoidance of arguments over points of dispute, an awful lot of bother for a twelve guinea bet.

Some commentators have argued that they refer back to an existing set of laws but this is doubtful. 'The ball caught, the striker out' – 'touch the umpire's stick' to complete a run – for a run out 'the wicket must be put down with ball in hand' – pitch length of 23 yards – twelve a side: nothing is assumed, as it might well have been if uniform laws had been in existence. These articles are trying to combat what was self-evidently a somewhat diverse, indefinite situation. A reasonable alternative explanation is of men who had a very rough idea of the generality of cricket but, when it came to high stakes, had to make decisions about fundamentals which for these two matches included the number of players, the length of the pitch, how to score a run and a refusal to allow run outs from a direct throw.

In 2009 Martin Wilson plus Martyn and Jeremy Butler valiantly translated a Latin manuscript dated 1723 found resting in the East Sussex Record Office.[13] In mock-heroic poetic style *Clava Falcata Torsio*, 'Playing ball with a curved bat'. Even in this pick-up game between two lines of 'true friends', there is a wager of £100 riding on the result. Nothing is standardised. The fielders are deployed, rounders style, behind the bowler, for instance. Most significantly, 'clothes are laid out and rules agreed.' In many sports, football among them, this issue of agreeing rules beforehand persevered into the modern era.

A rational interpretation of the Richmond/Brodrick document is that it was one of several such documents drawn up almost every time a match was played. It was only towards mid-century that gentlemen tried to find some overall acceptance of a central set of laws. Interestingly, this happened about the same time in three different sports and with some sense of sameness across the three, particularly in respect of the control of gaming. These were the formal establishment of the Jockey Club in 1750, the 1743 Broughton Rules, the first attempt to bring orderliness to pugilism, and the first cricket laws issued in 1744 by the very decisively titled 'Cricket Club'. This was based in London, with grandees urgently seeking some control mechanism amid the flux. The laws come to our attention though the medium of *The New Universal Magazine* of 1752 and the phraseology – 'play'd at the Artillery Ground, London' - is open to the inference that they were drafted for games at that particular venue which for a short while was the key arena for cricket.

How far the writ of these laws ran and how many of those playing cricket heard of or abided by them is a moot point. What they do emphasise is the concentration of involvement of London and the south eastern counties, predictable enough given that what would now be called the north-south divide was as much in evidence then as again it is today. All but a hundred or so of the 2000 or so matches known to have been played in the 18th century were staged in Essex, Sussex, Surrey, Middlesex, Kent and Hampshire.

The relatively small knot of wealthy and titled sponsors of cricket matches were chiefly from the home counties, most of them leaning towards London in their affiliations and life-style. As well as the Dukes of Richmond, based at Goodwood House in Sussex, and Alan Brodrick, Viscount Midleton at Peper Harow near Guildford in Surrey, there were the Sackville family, headed from 1720 by the Duke of Dorset, at Knole in Kent and Sir Horatio Mann in the same county, along with the Earl of Tankerville at Mount Felix, Walton-on-Thames, Surrey. Where town teams flourished they were often backed by the nobility, the Duke of Richmond's support of the Slindon side being an example.

The gentry did not hesitate to turn to the simple folk when wagers were involved. It was a natural progression. As well as grooms multitasking as jockeys, there were footmen featured in 'pedestrian' or running events. Footmen, properly so-called, had to be fleet of foot, as one of their jobs was to lope ahead of the coach to announce his master's forthcoming arrival. Thus the first paid cricketers earned their money indirectly, that is, as part of their ongoing wage and board. Thomas Waymark, 'the Father of Cricket Professionals', was apparently a groom on the Goodwood estate, although there must have been many an aristocratic eyebrow raised when Lord John Sackville chose his head gardener at Knole, Valentine Romney, to captain his lordship's Kentish XI. Lord John presumably took the view, one long suppressed in English cricket circles, that one should turn for advice to the best-qualified candidate, whether runs or roses were the subject in question. John Minshull, while an employee of the Duke of Dorset, scored the first ever recorded century, playing for the Duke's team in 1769. Charles Bennett, 5th Earl of Tankerville, assembled around him a fine array of cricketers: among them were the feared bowler, 'Lumpy' Stevens who was one of his gardeners, Joseph Miller who was his gamekeeper and William Bedster who was his butler.[14]

One internal piece of class distinction became evident and it is worthy of mention for it remained a constant into modern times. The nobs were not too keen on bowling. On the whole, they preferred 'Lumpy' Stevens and his plebeian mates to toil away with the hard graft while the gentlemen whacked away stylishly. The image of the foil-wielding lordling and the ploughman trundler was forever imprinted. That said, and as the ever empathetic David Underdown reminds us, the nobility and gentry did gallantly expose themselves by failure to the derision of crowds befuddled by drink and disappointed by lost bets,

Of course, it was not long before sinecurism set in. Rather like the later mode of counties giving impecunious amateurs posts as assistant secretaries, the gambling peers and gentry found estate appointments for promising cricketers. The talented James Aylward was bailiff for Sir Horatio Mann. We are informed that he was 'a poor one'. It was but a short step before a group of cricketing artisans started to operate more independently. While reasonably well-paid on a match basis of a guinea for a major fixture, rising as the century wore on to, exceptionally, a pay out of five guineas for a win and three for a loss, it is unlikely that any of them provided for themselves solely from cricket. They were chiefly men with itinerant trades adaptable to what were the fairly rare call of cricket which, in any event, was then cramped into a brief spell of early summer before the coming of the busy harvest weeks. Still, the average agricultural wage was only ten shillings (50p) a week, so the lure of earning just over twice as much from a day's cricket was enticing.

It should be stressed that not all the games were team-based. Matches with one, two or three a side were extremely popular and, as with the sides-orientated matches, bets were being laid throughout play, not only on the result but, as in today's spread betting, on passages of play and individual feats.

It was all tempting enough to attract corruption, not unexpectedly so, given that the whole of Hanoverian society and politics was riddled with bribery and patronage. Some of the early sets of cricket rules alluded to gambling and how it should be regulated. This small troupe of professionals would foregather at the Green Man and Still in Oxford Street, London, ready to be hired and, on occasion, bribed. A colourful example was the dilemma faced by the Nottinghamshire and All-England cricket teams at Lord's in 1817 in a match that had been apparently sold on both sides. It would require Lewis Carroll adequately to relate the confrontation of batsmen trying to get out and bowlers striving not to take wickets. Bribery was an element in all sports subject to wagering. The mix of betting and fixing is a lethal one and it proved to be a contributory factor in the violence and crowd troubles attached to cricket, as to other sports, when on offer as a public entertainment.

Lest it be thought that the 'simple' professionals were all to blame, it is right to cite the 'gentle' case of the unpleasant Lord Frederick Beauclerk who, despite being a clergyman and a son of the Duke of St Albans, claimed to earn some 600 guineas a season playing cricket, some of it in very dubious situations. It is interesting to note that, at the time when the first professionals were being paid, there was at least one 'shamateur' in the field.

In turning next, with this preliminary backdrop in mind, to the chief *motif* of this text, the hundred or so years of the amateur/professional relationship, we shall expect to meet a few more 'shamateurs' amid the anomalies of a not always clear-cut system.

1. G.M.Trevelyan *English Social History; a Survey of Six Centuries* (1944).
2. Robert Malcolmson *Popular Recreation in English Society 1700-1859* (1973) This is an excellent and well-researched of how English people really did spend their leisure time in the 18th century.
3. Most readers will be familiar with these valued tillers in the field, to which should be added the name of the diligent Ian Maun *From Commons to Lord's, vol I 1700-1750* (2009) a very thorough collation of 200 cricketing mentions.
4. Felipe Fernandez-Armesto *Civilisations* (2009) This is the most persuasive analysis of the multi-focal hypothesis.
5. Johann Huizinga *Homo Ludens; a Study of the Play Element in Culture* (1938) Possibly the most compelling account of the universalism of 'play'.
6. H.S.Altham *A History of Cricket; from the Beginning to the First World War* (1926) and Rowland Bowen *Cricket; a History of its Growth and Development throughout the World* (1970) are two seminal tomes that together lay the foundations for the continuing discourse on cricket's origins.
7. Peter Wynne-Thomas *The History of Cricket; from the Weald to the World* (1997) and John Eddowes *The Language of Cricket* (1997) offer the most reasoned and measured contributions to the ongoing debate about origins.
8. Richard.Cavendish The Death of Frederick, Prince of Wales *History Today*, March 2001.
9. John Adamson *The Noble Revolt; the Overthrow of Charles I* (2007) An acclaimed revisionist thesis on the primarily political character of the events leading up to the English Civil Wars of the 1640s.
10. J.H.Plumb *Penguin History of England in the 18th Century* (1950) – still regarded as perhaps the most succinct introduction to the study of this century.
11. David Underdown *Start of Play* (2000) These and later paragraphs owe a debt to this distinguished book, by a country mile the most clinical and yet the most attractive text on cricket in London and the surrounding counties during the 18th and early 19th centuries.
12. Thomas Hughes *Tom Brown's Schooldays* (1857).
13. Martin Wilson and Martyn and Jeremy Butler 'Clava FalcataTorsio or Playing Ball with a Curved Bat' *The Cricket Statistician* no.148 Winter 2009.
14. Underdown op.cit. For much in these paragraphs on both 'gentle' and 'simple' individuals, although David Underdown sunnily accents the enjoyment had rather than the money made more than does the more disgruntled current writer.

Chapter Three
Diaspora; Cricketing Migration

The advent of the modern, nationally uniform sport of cricket arrived flying, as it were, on two wings. One was professional and the other amateur and, by those tokens, they could also be characterised as lower class and middle or upper class. Initially more distinct, they gradually fused both in regard of spectators as well as players, although, intriguingly, class identity was never lost within that fusion.

The coming of this new model of cricket followed a phase in which cricket as a public entertainment had collapsed. At best, this might be viewed as a breathing space wherein cricket shrugged itself free of parlous attributes and advanced. At worst, it was a near-death experience. This modern version of cricket, prominent from about the beginnings of the Victorian era, had sufficient links with the past as to make the chain a recognisable one, yet the alteration was fundamental enough to hint at brand-newness. The changes were, *inter alia*, in technique, incidence, organisation, regulation and, above all, tone.

The decline of cricket was substantive. From 1720 there had been an annual average of some twenty matches retrospectively defined as 'important'. On reflection, that figure of no more than one or two a week during the season should remind that 'important' cricket was restricted in quantity as well as place. Nonetheless, the famine that ensued made these decades seem like years of plenty. Between 1802 and 1840 important matches never reached double figures in a summer. There were only two such fixtures in each of 1803, 1814 and 1818; there was only one in each of the years 1802, 1811, 1812 and 1813. 1841, with eleven fixtures, broke the dearth and pointed to a happier future.

The restricted ambit of these games both demonstrated the continuing dominion of the wider London region as well as its failure to export the game very much elsewhere in the kingdom. Of the 'important' 115 games – just five or six a season - played between 1801 and 1822 inclusively, 82, that is 71%, were played at Lord's. Most of the remainder were staged elsewhere in the south-east. After 1817 Cambridge hosted five games, a nod towards the provenance of the newer establishment emerging.[1]

Rowland Bowen quotes an 1813 newspaper in the Midlands attesting that 'the game had died there because it had not been played for some time', this being the first mention for three years. Hambledon, most notable of the few clubs outside London that had developed and staged major matches, had closed for business. The club minute book for 25 September

1795 tersely states 'no gentlemen present', leaving one to ponder the *Marie Celeste* poser as to whom then bore witness and penned this enigmatic phrase.

Commercial ventures had not been universally profitable. The Artillery Ground on Chiswell Street, London, where the cash-starved Honourable Artillery Company was keen to make some money, earns it place in cricket history as being probably the first venue to charge entry to all attending for a great match. This was in 1744 and it cost twopence. Several thousand were attracted but when the price rose to sixpence the crowd numbered only 200. The ground was let to and managed by the landlords of the conveniently neighbouring Red Horse pub but although all sorts of other events were on offer – foreshadows of tomorrow - it was difficult somehow to make a profit. George Smith then the landlord was declared bankrupt in 1748 and no major spectator cricket was played there after the 1750s.[2]

The retail exploitation of cricket proved at this time and into the 19th century to be something of a disaster. Entrepreneurs in provincial towns such as Leicester, Brighton, Leeds and Sheffield built enclosed grounds, hopeful of staging games, renting out the venue to local clubs, widening the range of activities, attempting to assemble membership lists and selling alcohol. None were uniformly successful for long. Even where they were profitable, the businessmen involved found, like Thomas Lord, that prime land brought a lucrative reward as urban development expanded. Perhaps most telling of all, Peter Wynne-Thomas has astutely calculated that by 1830 there were only a score of cricket professionals in the country, a huge decrease from, say, the fifty years before. He asserts that modern professionalism, defined as a full-time summer job, dates only from this point.[3]

Thomas Lord, like his fellow entrepreneurs, had opened his famous ground to such exotic events as pedestrianism, ballooning and pigeon-shooting in order to turn a profit. Four 'great' cricket matches a year was not a business-like proposition. He had moved twice under the threat of urban development and in 1825 he decided to sell his lease for building but the wealthy William Ward, himself no mean batsman, stumped up (apt slang usage) £5000 and presented MCC with the property.

It should be called Ward's ground. That £5000 ensured that the upper middle-class faction and interest would have a doughty stronghold when cricket was revivified.

It has been argued that the Revolutionary and Napoleonic War was the disruptive cause of this slowdown of cricket. This may have been the case although the sole close-up pressure had been the very brief point in 1805 when a Napoleonic invasion had been feared. As usual, in war as in peace, the rich notables who backed and gambled on cricket appeared to remain affluent enough, with some merchants doing exceedingly well. There are always ups and downs but, for instance, the armaments, textiles (all those uniforms) and victualling businesses profited from the hostilities. It should not be forgotten that the 18th century, during which cricket had dug something of a foothold in the south-east, had seen countless years of warfare along with much internal upheaval which, admittedly, continued into the first decades of the subsequent century.

Other sports seem not to have been unduly affected. The British prize-fighting championship, with James Figg its first winner in 1719, went on unabated, with, for example, the popular Tom Cribb adding the world title to his British one in the early 1800s. In 1879 James Rice, a racecourse journalist, wrote 'for some 200 years the pursuit of horse racing has been more attractive to our countrymen than any other outdoor pastime'. It stood up to the rigours of war with some pomp. Two of the five classics – the Two Thousand Guineas in 1809 and the One Thousand Guineas in 1814 – were actually launched during the wars. They followed swiftly the inaugural St Leger, 1776, the Oaks, 1779 and the Derby,1780, proof that, as *Whyte's History of the Turf* proudly claimed in 1840, 'for nearly a century and a half, the 'turf' has formed a favourite amusement for Kings, Lords and Commons'. Horse-racing was well established as the major national sport.

So how is one to explain this disastrous, near-fatal misadventure of cricket? First, it must be emphasised that one is drawing a distinction between 'formal' and 'generic' cricket. The former was the slightly more official game, with rules accepted by sufficient to enable gambling to occur and for crowds to gather able to find intelligible what they were betting on and watching. The 'generic' title refers to whatever mass of bat, ball and target pastime around the nation used that name. Like football at the time, it had as many versions as the bands of boys and young men who occasionally played it. Rowland Bowen correctly writes of 'unofficial laws' that 'enshrined local variations of long standing' into the 19th century and that in the preceding century 'differing versions of the game were played in different parts'.[4]

Second, on closer look at the evidence, it might be surmised that 'formal' cricket never quite became as fully grounded as, for example, horse racing in this its first manifestation. It was more a craze, a freakish gambling mania that suited the hour and then was almost gone. It is interesting that the newspaper coverage of those great games had more print directed at the betting than at the scores; while the word 'form' was borrowed from horse-racing as an indicator to readers how best to lay their cricketing bets. For a number of reasons, some of which will become more apparent later in the text, the gambling madness petered out, certainly in terms of wagering on practically everything. Establishment backs were being turned on the violence and venality associated with crowds at sporting events. Of course, betting remained a foremost component of horse racing. The sport of kings retained the loyal support of the ranks of blood and wealth and its regime of control was firmly entrenched.

Those enclosed cricket grounds that were developed prospered for a while and then fell empty, not unlike bingo halls in the late 20th century, although - if Lord's and Trent Bridge can bear the cultural comparison with the bingo-callers' jolly cry of 'legs eleven'– one or two in both cases carried on to keep afloat the concept. The salvaging of Lord's was a blessing for the future of cricket. MCC retreated behind its sturdy fences and hunkered down as if hibernating until the spring of clean-cut modern cricket appeared. The entry price was raised to sixpence in the knowledge that, as at the Artillery Ground, this would detract the rumbustious elements, leaving a smaller and more docile scattering of spectators. The bookmakers who had cried the odds so freely were banished, as the money-lenders had been driven from the temple in the scriptures. Wagering, excess alcohol and ruffianly behaviour were erased. In 1822 Benjamin Aislabie became the first secretary of MCC and his was to be an influential reign. He was one of those who imparted a new look and temper to cricket as a national pastime.

His contribution, patently, would be concerned more with the 'gentlemen' flank of the novel order. It was, however, on the 'players' side that the chief impetus came in respect of the national spread of refreshed 'formal' cricket. With an irony with which history frequently teases its adherents, this secondary success came directly from a primary failure.

William Clarke was certainly not a gentleman. He was a bricklayer, but he had added the sharpened arrow of underarm leg-spin to his income-flow quiver. Born in 1798, he married late but advantageously. An outrageously politically incorrect aphorism once advised that the perfect marriage for a male was to a silent beauty who owned a pub. Reports as to whether Mary Chapman, landlady of the Trent Bridge Inn, Nottingham, was loquacious or lacking in charm is not vouchsafed to us, but William won her heart and property. They married in 1837 and contrived to obtain use of and enclose the land adjacent to their hostelry as a cricket ground.

The omens were not good. Other cricketers had or were to try this combine of the ground and public house but with mixed fortunes. Daniel Day in Southampton and William Lillywhite in Brighton ventured and foundered, rather as had the landlords of the Red Horse apropos the Artillery Ground. Today we are well attuned to buying tickets for services. Then it was most uncommon. Although one of the distinctions between 'gentle' and 'simple' was that a few of the former might have paid to sit in a temporary stand (although watching from one's private carriage was also a possibility) to avoid mixing too closely with the many of the latter, sport was free. Profit came from drink and refreshments, hence the role of publicans as sponsors.

The use of the word ticket as in exchange for a service comes surprisingly late; it was not employed until the end of the 17th century and then only sparsely. One constant problem was the slowness of handling hand-written tickets, like those used for stage coaches, in respect of cricket matches when high numbers were crowding in to an event. Indeed, the railways found this difficulty insurmountable until in the 1840s Thomas Edmundson, the redoubtable station-master at Newcastle, invented the first automatic, pre-printed ticket machine, an unassuming mechanism that also in time eased the administrative difficulties of the leisure industry both in and outdoor.

What William Clarke and his fellow-entrepreneurs discovered was that generations of gratis entertainment had built a shyness about payment to watch. Nottingham's cricket-lovers were used to watching cricket on the Forest racecourse. Theirs was, so to speak, free love. Cricket's William and Mary did not prosper as they had hoped. 'The crowds', says Derek Birley, '...were not flocking to Trent Bridge'. Even though approaching his own half century, the intrepid bowler placed his son-in-law in charge of the ground and headed for London, where he, much remarked on as a canny bowler, joined the Lord's ground staff.[6]

At that time MCC offered employment to ten bowlers. It was a limited but solid job with MCC proving extremely loyal to these men. William Lillywhite was still on the Lord's staff when he died suddenly aged 62. The bread and butter work was practice for MCC members with sessions on Tuesday, Wednesday, Friday and Saturday during May, June and July – August found the gentlemen heading to the grouse moors. It was the closest then to being a full-time professional but, for William Clarke, the pay was inadequate. At the close of the 1846 summer, with MCC members dispersed to shoot game, William Clarke mustered an eleven to play three matches against odds in Manchester, Sheffield and Leeds. It would be a century and a bit before Kerry Packer was to have the same bright idea.

William Clarke called it the All-England XI (AEE). In previous generations random teams had been labeled 'England', just as club and sponsored sides had played under county banners, all aimed at attracting spectators. In 1826, for example, the Wellesbourne club sometimes played as 'Warwickshire.' William Clarke's eleven did have a much more rational claim to its title. Five of that initial team were from the MCC staff, so the bowling was taken care of by the best available. They were joined by the likes of Fuller Pilch, reckoned to be England's premier batsman, and Joseph Guy, another prominent bat of the day. For years this high standard was maintained. What is perhaps interesting from the viewpoint of a study aimed at class analysis is William Clarke's wily decision to include two amateurs, the very gifted Alfred Mynn, the giant Kentish star and the lesser known if more lengthily named Rev. Villiers Shallet Charnock Smith. Invaluable as he was as a player, Alfred Mynn, along with one or two other gentlemen, was indispensable for the social aspects of the tours, which often involved the meeting with and greeting of local dignitaries, especially where fixtures had been arranged at stately homes. Nicholas Felix, also of Kent and of gentle birth, was soon drafted in as Alfred Mynn's coeval for this purpose; like the other, he was an extremely fine cricketer. One must assume that, in the amateur tradition, they received liberal expenses.

The need for polite glad-handing reflected the enormous impact made by these 'warriors', as they were often nicknamed, with William Clarke branded 'our General'. Red carpets were unrolled, junketing was opulent and communities were enraptured by the visit of what, after all, was the nearest to a national team for any sport that had ever been witnessed. They played nine games in 1847, 17 in 1848...and 34 in 1851 and always more than twenty a summer until 1880. This was no flash in the pan.

For 34 years the AEE travelled the length and breadth of Britain, bringing cricketing succour to the masses.

The AEE was not a co-operative. William Clarke paid his players £4/£6, inclusive of expenses, a game, much the same as the MCC rate, although one or two players preferred the more sedate existence of Lord's as opposed to the often irksome travel of the wayfaring life. William Clarke was very much the boss. He insisted on a down payment of £70 from those offering opposition plus part or whole of the gate money, so he was always in the clear by £10 or £20 after wages, basically his only expense, had been met, even if the fixture was rained off or otherwise affected. A conservative estimate would be that his AEE profits were easily £1000 a season, putting him straight into the middle class bracket as per finance if not *finesse*.

Although by 1846 and thereafter the incidence and repute of cricket were, for reasons that the next chapter will explain, already on an upward curve, it cannot be doubted that the AEE played a significant role in the consolidation of an officially acknowledged construction of cricket and, over more than a generation, improved standards of play considerably. Peter Dark, a thriving equipment maker and supplier at a time when accoutrements like pads and gloves were coming into play alongside bats, wickets and balls, found to his delighted amazement that his wares were being ordered from the remotest parts of the kingdom.

Indeed, so numerous were the calls for travelling cricketers that copycat versions were established without any inroads into William Clarke's profits. John Wisden and others recruited the United All-England XI, which occasionally played a grand match versus the originals; there was a short-lived United North England XI and there was also a successful United South England side, started by Edgar Wilsher but to benefit mightily from the exploits of W.G.Grace. The redoubtable George Parr took up the reins of the AEE when William Clarke laid them down and proved to be a worthy successor, dominating the professional scene in these later years. Altogether this joint enterprise supplied the staple earnings to the first fully-fledged cadre of English cricket professionals and it was from this corps that the first overseas ventures to North America and Australia were recruited.

Towards the end of this phase there were even a couple of Clown teams on the road. This offers us an insight into the social crucible of the time when, in quickly changing conditions, there was a rash of entertainments being conveyed to settlements, many of them linked for the first time with improved transport but as yet not having developed their own established theatres and other venues, The Exhibition XIs were not alone on the highways and, increasingly, the railways of the nation.

As Little Nell and her feckless grandfather journeyed aimlessly in Charles Dickens' *The Old Curiosity Shop* (1840/41 but set in 1825), they encountered travelling entertainers. There among others were Mrs Jarley and her mobile waxworks and Short and Codlin, the puppeteers.

The eponymous hero of *Nicholas Nickleby* (1838) was enrolled as an actor-writer with the Vincent Crummles peripatetic theatre company. It is likely William Clarke bumped into non-fictional 'fit-up' Thespian troupes on his cricketing safaris. In the wake of Philip Astley's equestrian riding show dating from 1768, circus had also come to town, with, as well as several static venues, including Nottingham, Leeds and Birmingham, an outcrop of the tented variety.

The Leeds Amphitheatre had accommodation for 3000. Later the sea-side resorts would have resident circuses. In 1826 there came a brash American challenge of circus within a huge marquee. William Batty led the British response with a big top that held 1400 and, along with travelling fairs, the visiting circus remained very popular for generations.

Another example is well illustrated by the biography of Marie Tussaud (1761-1850). She inherited her uncle's wax exhibits and was instructed by him in the arcane craft of wax modelling, and in the macabre chore, while imprisoned, of making death masks of victims of the Guillotine during the French Revolution. Moving to England, she toured, a real-life Mrs Jarley, for 33 years before setting up a permanent home for her growing collection in Baker Street in 1842, inclusive of Napoleon's toothbrush and one of the teeth presumably cleansed by it.

Notable actors, circus performers and cricketers were welcomed, recognised and feted on these periodic often annual visits, usually with a similar mix of audience, many from the lower orders but always a goodly sprinkling of their so-called betters. In Thomas Hardy's *Far from the Madd'ing Crowd* (1874) Squire Boldwood sits with Bathsheba Everdene in relative comfort amid their servants and farm workers to watch an enactment of the story of Dick Turpin at a travelling fair. Unashamedly, the itinerant cricketers labeled themselves 'Exhibition' elevens, for in the nicest sense they were making an exhibition of themselves and becoming household names, with portraits on sale and many of the other trappings of celebrity.

In short, the professional cricketer found himself for the first time cast as an integral part of the entertainment industry, operating on a national basis.

Although this first modern cadre of 'pros' was almost entirely working class in origin, there was, within that massive social swathe, a quality they chiefly shared. They tended to come from an artisan rather than a labouring background. As with the paid occasional players of the past, cricket was still a part-time job. With the Exhibition elevens it became a full-time summer occupation, but to borrow the pained cry of the seaside landladies faced with lodgers complaining about high charges, 'we've got to think of the winter when you've gone.' It is well known that many early professionals were piece workers, able, for instance, to combine their lace making or other crafts at home with forays into paid cricket now and then, unlike others tied to the more stringent regimen of the farm or, increasingly, the factory.

One may also conjecture that the artisan, more used to selling his skills or wares and dealing with middlemen or customers, may have had or learned habits of confidence and social awareness that informed both their cricketing attributes and their deportment as paid entertainers. Among William Clarke's first wandering compatriots were Tom Box, a cabinet maker doubling as a wicket-keeper; the famed batsman Fuller Pilch who was a tailor; Joseph Guy, elegant bat and, one trusts, accomplished baker; William Hillyer, a quick bowler of note who was a gamekeeper; and William Martingell, medium paced bowler, also a gamekeeper but a shoemaker, too. Later recruits – the AEE, of course, continued its peregrinations after William's Clarke's death – were Edgar Willsher, fast bowler who came from farming stock and Julius Caesar, a fine bat who was a carpenter and painter by trade. George Parr, a major influence in these cricketing enterprises, was the son of a farmer; George Anderson, a powerful hitter, was one of the better educated of paid cricketers, while H.H.Stephenson, who excelled as batsman, bowler and wicket-keeper, became in later life a church warden and one of the Rutland market town of Uppingham's Poor Law Guardians.[7]

Sad to say, some of his comrades ended up in dire need of the never too kindly poor law. Julius Caesar, George Anderson and William Martingell were numbered among those, like, incidentally, many from the bottom rungs of the acting and circus professions, who died in reduced circumstances. Others did well, often as publicans, such as Tom Box and Joseph Guy. They were neither the first nor the last of sportsmen to be, as it were, called to the bar. However, the key issue was the relative good standing of these nascent professional cricketers among their own class. That precedent was to have, as will be later detailed, an influential bearing on the blending of gentlemen and players in the coming decades.

At much the same time the gentlemen were themselves engaged in their own missionary tours throughout the country. The amateur equivalent of the AEE began a year earlier in 1845 when four Cambridge students inaugurated I Zingari, from the Italian 'the Gypsies', a typically arch undergraduate conceit. The residential life of public school and Oxbridge made for fast friendships that were constantly being sundered first by vacations and then by widespread home addresses. I Zingari would provide the opportunity for such distant friendships to be sustained. The foursome contacted a score of their close buddies with the notion of a homeless and subscription-less cricket club of a very exclusive kind, open by invitation only. They would gather from the four corners at their opponents' ground. Within a year or two their fixture list was a healthy one and their exploits were published in the cricketing prints and annuals.

As with the AEE, there were copyists. Quidnuncs (1851), the Harlequins (1852) Free Foresters (1856) and Incogniti (1862) were among the first and the most notable. Significantly, one of I Zingari's first games was at a country house, the home of J.G.Sheppard in Suffolk. One or two noblemen – the Earl of Stamford and Warrington at Enville Hall, near Stourbridge and Lord Henry Paget in Staffordshire are examples – continued the old-style sponsorship of paid cricketers and supported the AEE but there was a general turning of the landed gentry towards its own kind. Country house cricket came into its own, often with a county seat organising a week's cricket, with visits from the glittering wandering sides among the highlights.

It quickly became as indispensable for a stately home to have a cricket ground in the 19th century as to have a swimming pool in the 20th. Eric Snow, dauntless researcher, identified sixty country house pitches just in Leicestershire and Rutland, along with eleven minor occasionally used sites.[8] This was no superficial aristocratic jolly. It was often extremely serious cricket for the leading amateur players of the nation. Hundreds of games were played, summer after summer, in a format that endured until the First World War. Writing in 1918 C.K.Francis, an Oxford blue and occasional Middlesex fast bowler recalled 'we used to stay in various country houses for about a week, playing two or three matches sometimes against very good teams. The cricket weeks at Preston Hall, Croxteth, Lees Court, Scarborough, Hothfield, Compton Verney, Wilton, Rood Ashton, Patshill, Northernwood, Escrick, Southgate, Vice Regal Lodge are only a few I remember out of the many.'[9] It is a possible there were a thousand such locations in the United Kingdom generating a gaudy moving carnival of amateur cricket over some half a century and more.

It is apparent, too, from the researches of Eric Snow and others that many of these grounds were frequently made available to the local village or township team rather than them lying idle for all but the special week. It was not unusual for the young gentlemen of the house to join, even if condescendingly, in some of those lesser fixtures. One or two peers, passionate about cricket, kept up the Hanoverian tradition of employing professional cricketers. The Earl of Stamford, for example, employed seasoned professionals at Enville Hall from 1845 to 1864, beginning with Reuben Roby and ending with Hiram Slack.

Even where the country house owners did not take their duties quite so seriously, they still required groundsmen to ensure the pitches were of high enough standard. The quality of groundsmanship matured over the century. One's week as cricketing visitor to a country house would be judged by the lavishness of the hospitality, the gaiety of the evenings' entertainment and the prettiness of the lady guests – and also by the excellence of the wicket. The nearest equivalent of the gentlemen who brought social graces to the working class Exhibition elevens were the hard-working groundsmen-cum-gardeners who made sure the wandering amateur sides played on carefully nurtured surfaces.

It was in these two ways, one cannily professional and artisan, the other fashionably amateur and gentlemanly, that modern cricket was introduced to and reinforced the length and breadth of Britain. It might be observed as a pincer movement encircling and suffusing the nation with the cult of cricket for all grades of society. This establishment of a sport, both national and cross-class in appeal, was made possible by a relatively abrupt change in both the socio-economic fabric and the cultural ethos of the United Kingdom. It is to this striking phenomenon that attention must now be turned.

1. Association of Cricket Statisticians *A Guide to Important Cricket Matches Played in the British Isles1707-1863* (1981) and *Complete First-class Match-List vol 1 1801-1914* (1996) and published after much hard toil, diligent endeavour and careful debate over several years.
2. Underdown *op cit* pp 95-97.
3. Wynne-Thomas *op cit* p.64.
4. Bowen *op cit* chap 5, particularly p.71.
5. Eric Midwinter 'Cricket's Near Death Experience' *The Journal of the Cricket Society* vol27 no 3 (2014) – for a fuller explanation of this phenomenon.
6. Derek Birley *A Social History of English Cricket* (1999) pp. 83-86.
7. Ric Sissons *The Players; a Social History of the Professional Cricketer* (1988) provides, among much useful material, valuable potted biographies of early professionals, pp 20ff.
8. Eric Snow *Country House Cricket Grounds of Leicestershire and Rutland* ACS Publications (1998).
9. Christopher Brookes *English Cricket* (1978) C.K.Francis's comment is quoted herein, p.145.

Chapter Four
Renaissance; The Revitalisation Of Cricket

'Between 1760 and 1850 the English ceased to be one of the most aggressive, brutal, rowdy, outspoken, riotous, cruel and bloodthirsty nations in the world and became one of the most inhibited, polite, orderly, tender-minded, prudish and hypocritical'.[1]

In one unequivocal and oft-cited statement the great social historian Harold Perkin incisively defined what amounted to a fundamental change in national character. In so doing he implicitly explained why and how cricket changed its ethical spots from Hanoverian black to Victorian white, literally in that a pure, creamy costume was adopted for playing purposes.

Whilst a comforting thesis that racial or regional character is in the blood and inherited genetically is still espoused, the speed of this change kyboshed any hope that nature rather than nurture was at work. The virile force that engendered so radical a change was cultural, not eugenic. It amounted to a reinvention of Englishness, a new strain to which cricket made an essential contribution and was at the same time moulded by it.

Jeffrey Richards, arguably the United Kingdom's principal cultural historian, has also shown how the English character differed in the Victorian age and the first half of 20th century compared with earlier times before about 1830.[2] We shall return later in the text to the findings of Professor Richards, for his analysis of a further change or rather relapse in the English psyche after the 1950s also had a major effect on cricket. Jeffrey Richards argues that two complementary tidal waves caused the first of these sea-changes. One was 'Evangelicalism' and the other was 'Chivalry'. In broad terms, the former introduced an earnestness of motive and aim into everyday life, while the latter cultivated the late 18th century notion of 'decency', interpreting it as a somewhat restrained courtesy.

The bedrock of Evangelicalism lay in the nonconformist or 'dissenting' tradition, including by this time the Methodists, the adherents of John Wesley but it also involved the 'low' churchmen of the Anglican communion, who opposed the less socially committed 'high and dry' wing. Anthony Trollope's *Barchester Chronicles* superbly dramatise this conflict. In *Barchester Towers*, published in 1857, Bishop and Mrs Proudie and Reverend Mr Slope represent the low and Archbishop Grantly and Reverend Mr Arabin the high sets. It is interesting that the epithet 'enthusiasm' was used to excoriate the Evangelical movement that proved to be a powerful instrument for social as well as theological change.

From the crusades to first halt the slave trade and next abolish slavery in British possessions to the campaigns to ameliorate working conditions especially for children, the Evangelical tendency was very active. It was to the fore in humanising state policy on justice. The number of often-brutal executions declined rapidly from over 500 in the years 1816-1820 to just 51 in the years 1836-40. This was in part because of judicial reforms, such as the abolition of many capital offences, but also in part because of a fall in the number of offenders in a less raucous national community. Public executions were banned from 1868. The chief reason was not out of kindness for the guilty party – a hanging behind closed prison doors was possibly more frightening – but to avoid the barbaric debasement of a vitiated mob.

The distinguished historian of the 19th century, Sir Robert Ensor, has asserted that 'no one will ever understand Victorian England who does not appreciate' that, among civilised communities, it 'was one of the most religious the world has known'.[3] This is certainly true in so far as attendance is concerned. After the indolence and apathy of the 18th century, the earnestness of the Victorian, in piety as in other matters, was distinct. It had a major behaviourial facet. The Victorians took the trappings and tokens of religion very seriously indeed. Thomas Arnold's model of 'the virtuous gentleman' is a lucid illustration of this solemnity of purpose – and it is important to underline how this affected both sides of the class barrier. His son the poet and critic Matthew Arnold said of the new breed of working men that they were 'at one in spirit with the industrial middle class.' Literary images of these two kinds might be observed in Elizabeth Gaskell's remorselessly upright mill-owner John Thornton in *North and South* (1854/55; and the only classical novel with the same title as a cricket fixture) and Charles Dickens' faithfully moralistic mill-hand Stephen Blackpool in *Hard Times* (1854).

A Census of Religious Worship showed that on Sunday 30 March 1851 11m people in England and Wales attended one of the nation's 35,000 places of worship, almost a half of them of the Anglican persuasion. There was one place of worship for every 700 of the population. What the Liberal politician John Morley was to call the 'ecclesiastical' effect, that is, the emphasis on the buildings, the funding and the membership of the church, rather than on the more purely religious element, was very pronounced. Churches were markedly involved in running schools but they also became engaged in recreational affairs of a musical, dramatic and sporting – cricket not least among these – nature.

The other element – Chivalry – mixed well with this Evangelical primness. Out of it grew the prototype of the decent and polite English gentleman. Literary references abound. One might cite Baroness Orczy's Scarlet Pimpernel (first staged in 1903, prior to publication in a novel sequence) or Jules Verne's Phileas Fogg in his *Around the World in Eighty Days* (1873). Cricketing aphorisms – it's not cricket, play a straight bat, keep the left elbow well up – are resonant of that ideal. Bruised by the rigours and discomforts of industrialism, the Victorians looked for solace in a largely non-existent pastoral past, one imbued with the quaint emblems of medievalism.

In any study of Victorian culture it is impossible to avoid this *faux*-medievalism. Historical novels such as Walter Scott's *Ivanhoe*, published in 1819; the 'vibrant medievalism' of Augustin Pugin's mock-Gothic edifices like St Pancras Station or the Houses of Parliament; sanitised folklore, the very word coined by the antiquarian William Thoms in 1846; political forays like the Young England movement, the Primrose League or Robert Blatchford's more left-wing best-selling *Merrie England* story; John Ruskin's Guild of St George, founded in 1878...the list is endless, as the nation luxuriated in 'the medieval dream'. The English taste for gardening – Walt Whitman called a trim lawn 'God's handkerchief' – was, and is, imbued with this nostalgic yearning. The hard-headed cricket groundsman of the age would probably have recalled what the grass was like when God had it on his own before the invention of the lawn mower by Edwin Budding in 1830 which led to the gradual disappearance of the scythe.

Fuller Pilch would have been enviously pleased; he carried a small scythe in his luggage against the rough-cut pitches his Exhibition eleven had sometimes to play on. The scythe was quite a long time a-vanishing. Until the Edwardian years the cricket ground at Loseley Park, near Guildford, home of the cricketing Christopherson family, was scythed by nineteen gardeners who rose at 4.00 a.m to be sure the pitch was prepared for country house cricket.

This combine of religiosity and pseudo-medievalism helped create the courteous and obedient conduct that became the fulcrum of English character during these times. A little later the headmaster of Harrow, Dr Cyril Norwood wrote 'for what has happened in the last hundred years is that the old ideals have been recaptured. The idea of chivalry which inspired the knighthood of medieval days, the ideal of service to the community which inspired the greatest of the men who founded schools for their day and for posterity have been combined in the tradition of English education today.'[4] Even as late as 1947 the medieval scholar, Ernest Barker, felt able to define the English national character as 'a mixture of stoicism with medieval lay chivalry'.

This, then, was the watchword not only of the ruling elite and the rural gentry but of the up-and-coming industrial and capitalist middle classes, for whom hard graft and conspicuous gain were the outward and visible sign of an inward and spiritual grace. It also boosted the motivation of that energetic and self-confident stream of young men, army officers, civil servants, clergymen, engineers and agriculturalists, who, not content with invading all parts of the nation, also took sail or steam and built an empire, an empire of which their cricketing credentials are perhaps its most enduring vestige. 'Who dies for England, sleeps with God', unctuously intoned Alfred Austin, who became Poet Laureate in 1896.

For three generations or more the yardsticks of personal and frequently professional conduct were of this fashion. Irrespective of one's inner disposition, it became customary for individuals from all social ranks to exhibit these mores. Some may have done so superficially, as 'mask' or 'caricature'. In many situations, including playing in a cricket match, it was a basic matter of social even vocational survival to abide by these norms.

The social changes from sinful rollicking to quasi-religious refinement were sudden in their happening. A crude Marxist analysis would interpret this novel intellectual and cultural 'superstructure' as being created by the underlying new economic 'structure'. A more refined opinion would discern a complex interactive mesh of influences.

Readers will be acquainted with the general lineaments of the Industrial Revolution that accompanied, influencing and influenced by, the perhaps less familiar cultural revolution described above. The pace and depth of change was breath-taking. A useful way of observing this phenomenon is to view it as three concentric and interconnecting rings of population, urbanisation and steam-powered factory-style production, a process tidily defined by the political scientist Herman Finer as 'congregation'.

Population had bobbed up and down unsteadily from medieval times. England's population was 5.2m in 1700. A demographic explosion shot this sky-high to 12m in the 1830s and then more than doubled it again to 30m by the beginning of the 20th century. Town-life grew exponentially. In the first half of the 19th century London's population doubled to 2m, while Manchester increased in size from 90,000 to 400,000 and Leeds from 53,000 to 172,000. Bradford saw an eight-fold increment from 13,000 to 103,000 and Blackburn sprang 500% to 65,000. When Queen Victoria came to the throne the majority of her subjects were rural dwellers; well before her demise the vast majority were, using the normal criterion of a settlement of a minimum of 5000 inhabitants, urbanised. These hordes were both labour-force and market for the burgeoning industrial economy. Under the impetus of steam power the factory system quickly evolved so that by 1850 the average number of workers per economic unit was 200. In 1782 Manchester, the world's first industrial city, had two mills; by 1800 it had 52 mills, plus 61 iron-foundries and machine shops. By the 1850s half the British work-force was engaged in the industrial trades.

A paragraph scarcely does justice to the enormity of the change. It is an essential facet of any study of modern sport to recognise that its canvas is this amalgam of a multitude of people cramped into busy towns and confined in large-scale work-places.

A specific aspect of this comprehensive nationwide change was transportation. The rapid development of the railways after 1830 is comfortably the most transformative event in the story of British social life. By the 1890s there were 20,000 miles of rail and 1,600m passenger journeys were annually negotiated. A near immobilised national community was liberated. The figure of four yearly public transport trips per individual in 1830 was mentioned in chapter one. By 1910 the ratio was 120 trips per individual. Tubes, buses and trams were also in the reckoning, totalling an amazing 5bn public transport journeys a year.

The effect of railways on cricket has been well-rehearsed.[5] W.G.Grace would have been a country practitioner with a regional repute as a sportsman had it not been for Paddington. The Exhibition XIs would have not by any means been so progressive and wide-ranging without these accommodating rail links – although the sport that benefited most from rail transport was horse racing. Before rail the horses had to walk from course to course, so they had to be of an age that provided stamina enough; only when they could be conveyed was it possible to have the one and two year old sprinters competing. It led to more courses, more, faster and shorter races, bigger crowds – and everyone, owners, jockeys, punters and especially bookmakers, was happy.

It is difficult to grasp the sheer scale of the cultural and socio-economic switches in British life. Cricket, reborn and fitted for this brave new world, emerged as a potent force, altered and boosted both by the alterations in cultural tone and the advantages accruing from industrialism and urbanisation.

It is something of a curio that the principal focus for the cricketing reformation was the public school. It was to be the *alumni* of the public schools, full of vim and ambition, who would be the carriers of the game not only within but also beyond British shores. The public schools themselves underwent a major reform which in an academic nutshell encapsulates what happened to the nation at large. They ceased to be the 'nurseries of vice', as Thomas Bowdler, the notable censor of Shakespeare, labelled them. They had exemplified the 18th century with displays of chaotic violence and horror. The worst 'sink' school in the most deprived district of the UK today looks serene in comparison; among the frequent riots there was one at Westminster School that had to be subdued by soldiers with fixed bayonets. The sturdy grammar schools of Elizabethan England had also fallen into extreme desuetude but, out of this slough of many dreadful schools there arose a few more enlightened establishments. Sometimes the neighbourhood suffered. Rugby School, founded in 1567 by a local grocer Lawrence Sheriff for local boys was superseded by a boarding establishment for rich teenagers, increasingly borne there from over a wide area by the convenient trains. It is from that long-forgotten charitable purpose of these ancient schools that the now rather misleading appellation of 'public' derives.

While Thomas Arnold for his reign at Rugby is rightly viewed as the seminal headmaster of the new regimes, his motto of 'Godliness and good learning' did not embrace sport too readily. It was his disciples – Edward Thring of Uppingham; C.J.Vaughan at Harrow; H.H.Almond at Loretto and E.W.Benson at Wellington are examples – who raised the standard of Athleticism. In particular, cricket became the physical touchstone for the public school *credo* that strove to catch the essence of evangelicalism and chivalry

Both as writer and protagonist, Thomas Hughes expounded the doctrine of 'Muscular Christianity', perhaps the closest to a creed that extolled the joint virtues of the evangelical-chivalric convention. It defined clearly the Victorian English gentlemen. In 1841 MCC, led by the amiable and corpulent Benjamin Aislabie, played at Rugby what was correctly described as an 'unfinished' rather than a drawn game. In recognition of its salient historical worth, MCC celebrated its centenary in the dark days of World War II in 1941. Thomas Hughes captained the school in 1841 and then made a set-piece of the game when disguised as Tom Brown in his semi-autobiographical story.

In the famous novel Tom and one of his *alter egos* Arthur (the 'Christian' one; 'Scud' East had the 'Muscular' role) discuss cricket with 'the young master'. 'What a noble game it is, too', says the teacher, to which Tom responds, 'but it's more than a game, it's an institution.' Arthur adds, 'it is the birthright of British boys, old and young, as *habeas corpus* and trial by jury are of English men'. 'The discipline and reliance upon one another it teaches,' claims the master. 'is so valuable...(it is) an unselfish game. It merges the individual into the eleven; he doesn't play that he may win, but that his side may'.

Cricket, once a rumbustious, occasionally tumultuous Hanoverian pastime, frowned upon by some even in that century of vulgar and ruffianly carryings-on, was suddenly the acme of ethical probity. The pedant might point the finger of criticism at the history teaching at Rugby if Arthur believed cricket had so lengthy a heritage but, then, it was already an aspect of the cult that the legend of longevity had to be promulgated. The 'young master' was George Cotton who soon became headmaster of Marlborough and later Bishop of Calcutta, the senior prelate in India. It is not irrelevant to an analysis of an emergent morality that George Cotton was to have married Thomas Arnold's daughter, Jane, but the nuptials were cancelled in the light of the prospective bridegroom's mother's affection for strong drink. The sympathetic reader will be comforted to learn that George Cotton found solace in the marital embrace of Sophia Ann Tomkinson, another churchman's daughter.

The public schools grew in strength and in numbers. There was a move to a starting age of thirteen, with younger boys tending to attend the new line of preparatory schools that were opened. A crucial element was the arrival of the sons of 'new money'. The merchants and factory-owners made abruptly rich by the Industrial Revolution proceeded to gentrify their families, to the disgust of, it must be said, Richard Cobden, central figure of the free trade movement and exponent of what was sometimes called Manchesterism. He deplored this aping of what he called the 'clod-pole aristocracy', believing that the wealth of the new middle class should be deployed in creating high-minded, forward-looking cities. He visualised Manchester as 'the Venice of the North'.

It is prototypical of the times that the 'shopocrats' turned backwards instead to the land and the pastoral fallacy. The very men who had built the industries were eager to play out the false anti-industrial 'medieval dream' of a rustic idyll. Robert Peel and William Gladstone are two famed examples of the sons of Lancashire trade moving through public school and Oxford and themselves – at Drayton Manor, Staffordshire and Hawarden respectively - living in stately homes. Among cricketers, A.N. Hornby, child of a Blackburn cotton mill owner, went to Harrow and briefly to Oxford and set himself up with a country estate, Parkfield in Cheshire.

Neville Cardus baptised him 'the Squire of Lancashire'. One with more modest cricket credentials – twelve first-class games for Hampshire – was Reginald Hargreaves, son of an Accrington calico printer. Educated at Eton and Christ Church, Oxford, he was established in a county seat, Cuffnells in the New Forest, although his celebrity status perhaps rests more on his marriage to Alice Liddell of 'Wonderland' notability.

However, the new middle classes whose wealth fuelled the expanding public school movement may have been snobbish but they were far from being stupid. Brass was brass. Their expectation of value for money was paramount. The stringent cleansing of the academic Augean stables owed much to their consumer consciousness. A sidelight on the introduction of cricket into the curriculum is that it could be domesticated. Much of what had passed for school games had been field-sports that took place outside the school and all games, including cricket, had been organised by the boys themselves. Gradually, the regimen of compulsory games supervised by the masters developed. It was never ideal; much pupil-led tyranny and bullying persisted but, compared to earlier times, it was as if Eden had replaced Hades.

It was largely pupils who had undergone this educational process who furnished recruits for the country house weeks and were, to some extent, when on their home patches ready to play against or sponsor the itinerant Exhibition XIs. Inculcated with cricket and taught to believe in its virtuous elements, they were anxious to continue playing after school. Wherever they went, they played and drew others, sometimes from among the lower orders, into the game.

There were four principal outlets for this enthusiasm. First, many of them went to Oxbridge and soon many of the colleges as well as the varsities themselves were fielding cricket teams. The crux of this pattern of cricket became the Varsity match. After a couple of such fixtures in 1827 and 1829, the series began in regular earnest in 1836. MCC and Oxbridge fixtures began in 1830.

Second, they returned to their own or other schools as masters and sustained the goodly tradition of schools cricket. By the end of the century there were about a hundred schools, inclusive of ancient public schools and the newer 'proprietary' schools, as they were known, together with a number of prestigious day schools. All of them made cricket a central part of their ethos. In mid-century there had only been about forty such schools. Some, like Eton and Harrow, were annually coupled for a gala match at Lord's; all eventually had a fixture with MCC every summer. From the 1860s onwards Old Boys teams were started, often with, as their titles - Eton Ramblers, Harrow Wanderers – suggest, something of the flavour of the amateur travelling elevens.

Third, many public school and Oxbridge former students were in holy orders and made cricket part and parcel of their ministry. As curates and parsons, they often encouraged and played for village and township teams in their parish, perhaps having a more direct linkage and over a wider geographical range with players from the lower classes than other groups of cricketing disciples. Of the 795 Oxford and Cambridge blues of the Victorian epoch, a quarter 209 in all, were ordained. At one time the sizable parish of St Mary's, Southsea fielded a full eleven just of curates.[6] Anthony Trollope in his 1884 novel *An Old Man's Love* described thus the 'exquisitely fatuous' Rev Montagu Blake as being 'not so strict in matters religious as to make it necessary for him to abandon any of the innocent pleasures of the world. He could dine out, play cricket and read a novel.'

At a time when Christian devotion was at its height and the acceptance and practice of faith was widespread, the relation of church and cricket was exceptionally strong across the classes. It became 'the Holy Game'. Reading the homilies and sermons of the age, one finds it sometimes difficult to decide which of cricket and religion is the metaphor for the other. The vision of 'the One Great Scorer' in the well-known Grantland Rice verse is but one illustration among hundreds of this absorbing relationship. Another instance is the Rev Thomas Waugh's *The Cricket Field of the Christian Life*, published in 1894, close to the high water mark of this sporting religiosity. God is the Captain-King, delighted that your 'innings' has left your conscience trouble-free, so that on 'resurrection morning' as you emerge from the pavilion you would be greeted with angelic cries of 'well played, sir'.

Fourthly, a considerable number of former pupils took commissions in the army which was, for a time, as big a purveyor of cricket as any other institution. In 1841 the order was issued that every barracks should lay and maintain a cricket ground. Former servicemen will wryly recall the chasm that often exists between the weighty military order from on high and its artful evasion on the ground. Nonetheless, cricket was by no means unknown in army circles and this edict did lead to its considerable expansion in the military world. There were many inter-regimental games, with the Woolwich and Sandhurst annual fixture the martial equivalent of Oxford v Cambridge.

From the standpoint of this text, a caveat must be entered about the dominant role of officers, at least in the major matches. In 1870, as one illustration, the initial-less Private McIntyre appeared as the sole other ranker alongside ten commissioned soldiers for the Household Brigade versus the Royal Artillery. One convention held good. Private McIntyre did most of the bowling and took ten wickets in the match. The ordinary soldier probably had to excel visibly to crash upwards through what might now be called the glass ceiling. Of course, inter-platoon games on these grounds for the rank and file would have been likely - but here again one must recollect the working of the military mind. The 1841 order commanded that the troops would be required 'to pay the estimated cost of repairs, as in the case of barrack damages.' The army's inhibiting response to that type of edict has been usually to insure against so dread an eventuality by keeping the article in question under wraps and never using it.

That weary hint of scepticism aside, the soldiers joined with the clergy, the school masters and the students to detonate what has been termed 'the Great Cricket Explosion'.[7] Its shock-waves were felt all over the country. All in all, an immense number of keen cricketers were in places and in posts conducive to spreading the word and the deed of the sport. Reformed cricket was, within a generation, a national sport of unblemished reputation.

1.   Harold Perkin *The Origins of Modern English Society* (1969).
2.   Jeffrey Richards *Film and British National Identity; from Dickens to Dad's Army* (1997), for an extended exegesis of this topic.
3.   R.C.K. Ensor *England; 1870-1914* (1936).
4.   Cyril Norwood *The English Tradition in Education* (1928).
5.   For example , see Eric Midwinter *The Cricketer's Progress; Meadowland to Mumbai* (2010) pp.94-98.
6.   Gerald Howat. 'Cricket and the Victorian Church' in *Cricket Medley* (1993) pp. 62-71.
7.   Keith A.P.Sandiford *Cricket and the Victorians* (1994), especially chapter 4, pp.53-79.

Chapter Five
Clubs And County Clubs

Cricket had become the visible and picturesque emblem of English life and character at that time – the phrase underlined mindful that, were the conditions to change, the emblem would be redundant. For then, and perhaps reaching a zenith in the 1890s, the nation and its chief sporting symbol enjoyed a symbiotic relationship.

The staple of the ubiquitous cricketing network was the club. There had been a few cricket clubs, with the necessary internal systems, in Georgian cricket circles but most cricket had been more random, relying on organisers and sponsors to promote games and select teams. The club, with its minute book, its annual general meeting and its elected officials, really came into its own in the Victorian era. It was a device which, from trades unions and friendly societies to choral groups and horticultural associations, penetrated every activity in every community. Especially after 1883, when the Boy's Brigade, first of the formal youth organisations, was started by William Smith in Glasgow, it would have been difficult to find a household where some if not all of its members, young and old, were not members of 'clubs' of one type or another.

In the sporting, as in other vogues, the club was the means of securing the 19th century ideal of 'rational recreation'. Responsible Victorians, beset by terrible public health problems and, following the publication of Charles Darwin's *On the Origin of Species* in 1859, looking over their shoulders at the 'survival of the fittest' slogan, became fitness fanatics. Athleticism was the keyword at school and afterwards. They were also drawn to the notion of the bureaucratic and systematic response – and this was manifestly true of both middle and working classes. The rash of cricket clubs was not a lone epidemic. The associationist contagion was rife. This point must be stressed that, given the flurry of cricket club formation, the higher ranks of society could not have provided the numbers to promote or support them in such profusion. That is not to detract from the major role played by the middle and upper classes. Their money and talent were invaluable. But the workers, particularly in the industrial trades, were also honing skills in the arranging of craft unions, co-operative societies and the like.

By the last quarter of the 19th century cities like Birmingham and Liverpool had well over 200 cricket clubs within their bounds.[1] Assuming that to be a standard distribution, it suggests that Britain at this time rejoiced in a cricket club for every 2/3000 of the population, with an estimated 15,000 in all, an intriguing figure given that England and Wales was divided into 15,000 parishes, but not forgetting Scotland and Ireland. From the heart of London to the remotest village outpost, cricket clubs were formed, and, viewed by churchmen, civic leaders, employers and other local big-wigs as a necessity rather than a luxury item, there were charitable grants and contributions available to guarantee viability. As Keith Sandiford affirms, 'cricket clubs were as vital to society as schools and churches.'[2]

In the more populous areas cups were placed on offer while associations - a noun favoured by the Victorians as the story of football bears witness – were formed. Just as 40 or 50 teams might compete for a trophy, a group of clubs might cluster together to arrange a regular fixture list. This device was the forerunner of the league, another appreciative nod to the footballing fraternity. The Birmingham and District League (1889) and the North-east Lancashire League (1890, later the Lancashire League), the North Staffordshire and District League (1890) and the South-east Lancashire League (1892, soon to be the more famous Central Lancashire League) were among the first, with Yorkshire and the other northern counties seeing similar groupings of what were usually a dozen to a score of clubs existing in a circle of roughly a 20 or 30 mile radius. It is worth noting that a man ticking almost all the amateur boxes the Rev J.R.Napier of Marlborough School, Cambridge University and Lancashire was the founding President of what became the Central Lancashire League.

A taste of the commercial ingredient entered into the league venture but not overly so, at least as far as obscene profit went. Few if any grew absurdly rich through bankrolling a league club. It was more the serious necessity of the enterprise that mattered. The early introduction of professionals, sometimes as many as four but over the years tending to be just one per team, was testimony to this more earnest approach and league cricket did provide a parochial loyalty and adherence that, for example, failed to characterise the outings of the Exhibition elevens.

Some clubs remained quite elitist; Hampstead, one of the leading London region clubs, charged members two guineas annually, sufficient to deter those not middle class in pocket and style. However, league clubs in industrial areas and village green sides in rural districts had in common a cross-class base and, unlike the bourgeois organisms such as Hampstead, had been consciously established on those lines. Necessity may, in the smaller hamlets, have been sometimes more the mother of inventive team selection if the local clergy and gentry could not muster eleven good men and true, but there is no doubting the sense of cricket as an improving tool for the lower classes. Cricket, with its kit and impedimenta, has always been a moderately expensive pastime; not so costly as horse racing or real tennis but more pricy than football. It has been calculated that the expense of equipping someone to play cricket in late Victorian England would have been over £2, which would have been the weekly wage of many skilled workers at that time. It is certain that many clubs outside the inner elite would have provided equipment other than boots and clothing such as bats, pads and gloves. That practice continued for several generations.

It was out of this amazing network of town, district and village clubs, in particular the more high-flying, exclusive middle-class variety, that the system of county cricket clubs arose. The precedents were there, albeit in haphazard fashion, for in Georgian times noble landowners who owned great tracts of a shire felt entitled to call any team representing them accordingly while often a town club when reinforced by neighbours for a special fixture had done the same. Hambledon *qua* Hampshire is an example. This tactic had been encouraged by artful taverners, bookmakers and newspaper editors, keen extravagantly to embellish the styling of a game for the purposes of their marketeering, just as similarly they had tended to exaggerate the size of wagers. The scrapings of so-called county cricket that had been sustained until early in the 19th century were likewise puffed by the sporting press doing its ingenious best to spot a county champion amid the bits and pieces.

It followed, therefore, that when the gentlemen in a given sector of the nation wished to raise local standards they chose to do so by a commitment to their shire for this purpose. It upheld a rather ramshackle tradition. It drew some often misleading cosmetic aid from the pastoral traits of the shire; a county name sounded more countrified than that of a city. Of most practical bearing, it leaned on what was the recognised ambit of the ancient divisions of British local government. Other sports, the football codes, athletics, hockey among them, also utilised or would utilise the county for the control and betterment of their activity, although most did so by forming an 'association', with occasional representative games or tournaments, rather than a participating 'club' *per se*.

Rather boringly from a literary stance, the county clubs were mostly formed in monotonously similar manner over a relatively short time. Not for county cricket the colourful assortment of football team origins with churches, schools, workplaces and whatnot engaged, including - Derby County – county cricket clubs. In county after county, delegates from the most prestigious clubs gathered, with yet another curtsey to tradition, in a tavern and agreed to set up a county club.

It was a messy process. Some counties had had primitive autonomy hitherto; some counties failed and started up again later or had distinctive changes of institutional format at some point; some counties established clubs which collapsed. Like the parable of the sower, some seeds fell on stony ground. Nonetheless, for all that there were counties with what in the parallel worlds of criminals and police officers would be termed 'previous' and others that tried and failed, the main bulk of the originating activity was in the last third of the 19th century. Moreover, at some time every county in England and Wales has boasted a *bona fide* county club, as have most of the counties of Scotland and Ireland, then, of course, not partitioned. Only three counties in the British Isles have not tried their luck with a county cricket club.[3]

A common denominator in the progress of county establishment, one affecting its class relations markedly, was the role played by the premier bourgeois clubs where the membership was restricted by price and/or social control. Some may have employed a professional or two, if only for practice or groundwork purposes. It was not like the league clubs that evolved in the industrial areas where the professional was, in some case, earning as much as some of his fellow working class team-mates who would have been barred from those more prestigious sides or found them unaffordable.

Thus the emergent county teams inherited this social structure. Carmarthenshire, for example, specifically ruled that tradesmen were ineligible for membership. The styling of some of the initial county sides did not beat about the bush of social correctness; 'the Gentlemen of Warwickshire', for instance, left the onlooker or newspaper reader in little doubt as to the sociological provenance of the eleven. Some counties evolved first as subscription clubs whereby the gentlemen paid a fee to fund a team with a more potent professional component for their personal diversion.

This general tendency was amplified by another common element in the county mix. In almost every case the formation of a county club was based not on some spontaneous amalgamation of that shire's leading clubs but on the controlling majesty of one such club, sometimes after a tussle with an equally powerful rival, Canterbury and Maidstone in Kent being an instance. Those whose attentive minds reach back to history lessons in chalky classrooms will appreciate the analogy of the Unifications of Germany and Italy which were negotiated about the same time as most of the counties were being properly founded. It was not so much a combustion of either German or Italian nationalistic fire that did the trick as the expansion of the powerful Prussia and Piedmont-Sardinia respectively dominating the prescribed area overall.

Lancashire provides a compact case-study of this phenomenon. The Manchester club was founded in 1818, possibly 1816, and, like other city-locked clubs had a move or two because of urban development before arriving at what was the second of two Old Trafford grounds in 1857. Some years earlier in 1842 Manchester visited Lord's and suffered a humiliating rout. Dismissed for 59, their attack 'was very deficient', according to one press report, 'it being of the old-fashioned underhand school, which afforded the MCC gentlemen much amusement in hitting it away' to the tune of over 200 runs. The crushed Mancunians forfeited the match and skulked back to their northern fastness. It show once again the varying standards of cricket in those days, for, although round arm bowling had been legalised in 1835, it was still not uniformly practised.

There follows a deliberate digression, albeit one that touches on the same point. In 1944, writing coincidentally in a Manchester newspaper, the usually perceptive George Orwell claimed that Charles Dickens knew nothing about cricket because in his one and only 'reference' to cricket he has Dingley Dell forfeit the game against All-Muggelton in *Pickwick Papers* (1837 but set in the 1820s) thus demonstrating he was 'ignorant of its rules'. Homer nods twice. First, there are at least sixteen 'references' to cricket in the main Dickensian canon of novels, as well as umpteen other mentions in his journalistic and allied writing. Second, if MCC acknowledged a forfeited match in 1842 it is likely Charles Dickens was aware of what, evidently, in some circles, was an acceptable mode.[4]

Manchester had learned a rueful lesson in the variations in cricketing habits and practices that still abounded in the 1840s. The club suffered another humiliation in 1846 when XVIII of Manchester were beaten on their then home ground in Hulme by an innings and 31 runs by William Clarke's AEE XI. The tale is told of the man losing his way *en route* to a Hallé orchestra concert in Manchester, A down-at-heel busker was stood in the gutter, cap at his feet awaiting the dropping in of coins, and playing the violin. 'How do you get to the Free Trade Hall?' asked the would-be concert-goer. 'Practice, son, just practice' answered the indigent fiddler.

The Manchester club took the violinist's sage counsel to heart and practised ardently. It began to use professionals – talented ones like Fuller Pilch, John Wisden and Fred Lillywhite – to strengthen the squad. Like other clubs, it was chiefly an internal operation, with members turning up to practice and play pick-up games and without a regular fixture list. Professionals were employed as bowlers and, by that token, coaches, while, a straw in the wind, members of neighbouring clubs were sometimes invited to join the revels under the heading of 'Manchester and District'. Results improved and incipient spectators attended.

Re-housed in a handsome new home and thriving, Manchester CC called a meeting at, typically, a hostelry, the Queen's Hotel in the centre of the town. It was scheduled for 12 January 1864 – slap-bang in the middle of the socio-economic crisis caused by the American Civil War and the dearth of cotton. Half a million textile workers were unemployed in the region and 'famine fever', as the Typhus that raged among starving families was called, had reached epidemic proportions. Some of the 34 gentlemen who attended the meeting must have walked past busy soup kitchens to reach their destination. Eleven were from the Manchester club and ten others from three other Manchester based clubs, plus four from the bustling Liverpool club. Thirteen clubs were represented but there was no one from the north of the county.

A county club was founded and a county team, often eked out with two or three professionals was fielded. Liverpool CC was inclined to take some part in the leadership but baulked at meeting the costs and underwriting the expenditure which was usually £120 a year. He who pays the piper... the *quid pro quo* of financing the operation was that all games were played at Old Trafford, where crowds of 300 or 400 were initially attracted, and that the Manchester committee should select the teams. Shrugging off the rivalry and envy that was a consequence, Manchester Men became the Gentlemen of Lancashire. In 1872, for example, Lancashire played six and Manchester 32 games, both with reasonable success. The team-sheets were virtually indistinguishable.

The reason the Manchester example is a neat one is because of the overt nature of the take-over. In 1880 the decision was taken to amalgamate the two clubs as 'the Lancashire County and Manchester Cricket Club'. It remained thus until well in the modern era. For some time until after World War II prestigious local clubs had home and away fixtures with 'Manchester Club and Ground' ('ground' as in ground staff) which was tantamount to Lancashire's 2nd XI.[5]

In no major case did a county, as in other sports, organise itself as an alliance of clubs. Rather did the counties appeal for individual members, hoping, as they genuinely strove to lift standards by raising a county banner, that the better players from surrounding clubs would join, as often they did. Apart from sometimes creating a barrier between the county club and the clubs that existed within the shire boundaries, it automatically fell to the dominant club to act as the Prussia or Piedmont-Sardinia in a county 'unification', with, to extend the analogy to its doggedly bitter end, usually a stalwart and competent individual cast in the role of Chancellor Bismarck or prime minister Cavour. A complementary factor was a sizable population base both for members and, gradually and importantly, spectators, with, of even more moment, the railway connections that were the prerequisite of Victorian county cricket. Realpolitik ruled with a heavy urban iron hand within a thinnish rural velvet glove.

Of the original 'Octarchy' of leading counties only Nottinghamshire, where the town team had been a stronghold, found its home just across the river boundary at Trent Bridge. As for the others, county towns like Lancaster, York, Gloucester, Lewes and Maidstone yielded to Manchester, Sheffield/ Leeds, Bristol, Brighton and Canterbury, while both Middlesex and Surrey opted for grounds that soon fell within the London local government boundaries.

Contemporary voices of a conservative tenor had ridiculed the Exhibition XIs and pleaded for more county cricket. In the wake of the glories of county cricket over the next couple of generations, some modern cricket historians have suggested that the continuance of both amateur and professional itinerant teams delayed the development of county cricket. The boon of hindsight may be at play in this conclusion, even allowing for the natural overlap of the travelling Exhibition and more static county formats. An alternative judgement might reverse the equation. It was not until the Exhibition and Country House teams had thoroughly accomplished the groundwork that there was sufficient quality and interest to launch a more studied county programme.

And it had a downside. It has often been said, doubtless with some truth, that county cricket offered the opportunity to devote one's affections devotedly to one's local team. Unluckily, even when it reached some enlarged regularity towards the end of the 19th century, this was quite a limited proposition. The north-east and, beyond Gloucestershire, the west went unserved; only in the 20th century did Durham and Glamorgan bring balm to the afflicted. Although the northern and later the midland counties attracted reasonable support from the industrial working classes, it was the lower orders who suffered most from top-class cricket starvation. They had neither the money nor the time to journey long distances to watch good cricket when, earlier, they had, even if only once or twice a summer, had it supplied on their own door step. Scotland is frequently scorned as lacking in a cricketing soul but perhaps that valuable possession was wrenched from the Scots by an absence of high-class cricketers on view.

W.G.Grace played fourteen minor games in Scotland, most of them in the cities of Glasgow and Edinburgh, mainly before 1877, then a gap in the meat of his career until a few more after 1890; none of them was what came to be judged first-class. The first international sporting star and the greatest cricketer was never seen in his pomp and against meaningful opposition north of the border. There was a sense in which the county cricket formula was inward-looking.[6]

It was not helped in that the club at the pinnacle of this pyramid with its base of local clubs and its medium tier of county clubs was a reluctant leader. Clothed in Georgian entitlement and very much an aristocratic bastion – in the 1880s when MCC's membership was over 2000, one in seven of these gentlemen were titled – the club was not much moved to act as final arbiter. Like Julius Caesar refusing thrice the imperial crown, MCC were unwilling to assume supreme authority, although MCC's stance was more genuine and less politically astute than Caesar's. Possibly the grudging disinclination of Oliver Cromwell to become king would be a more correct choice of historical equivalence.

Eventually, as the counties fumed and bristled over one controversy and then another, MCC were persuaded to adopt a supervisory role in regard and laws and regulations. Curiously, it would be 1898 before MCC headed up a Board of Control and the summer of 1899 was the first time MCC had oversight of team selection for all five tests as opposed to just the Lord's match. Actually, it would be 1907 at Sydney before the first match in the Anglo-Australian canon was one in which both sides represented sovereign states and were selected by acknowledged national agencies – the first true 'international' Test, leaving question marks over the status of the previous 76 so-called Test matches.

With its principal club loth to take the lead and its mainstream, that is, top-grade county, clubs few in number and inhibited in mind-set, these issues are important because they pose an awkward question. In this lengthy period of burgeoning county and Test cricket, to what extent was the mentality of the cricket authorities geared to the organisation of an evidently popular modern sport in respect of what in effect was, socially speaking, a two-tier audience?

Before addressing that poser head on, what can rightly be said about the evolving formula of mainline cricket was that it was providing more employment for the professional player. If the range of prime cricket watching for the masses narrowed, the employment opportunities for some fraction of that host opened.

Professional cricketers having been reduced to a beggarly twenty or so during cricket's decline around the turn of the previous century, MCC alone employed 60 ground bowlers by the end of the 19th century chiefly for the benefit of its members. Surrey had a ground staff of 32 and Lancashire more than twenty while Warwickshire and Nottinghamshire employed about a dozen each. The remaining first-class counties had fewer professionals; a guesstimate for the total number of paid cricketers in the upper tier of the game in the 1890s would be 200, ten times more than the 1820s. The warning note 'at any one time' must be added for the turn-over was rapid; possibly two-fifths enjoyed just one season of county employment, with no more than a luckier or abler fifth playing county cricket for over ten years.

Naturally, many of those not making the grade found cricket employment in the northern and midland leagues, while plenty of non-league clubs hired at least one professional. A common usage was to double up the playing side with groundsmanship, in some pleasing cases with the lure of a cottage beside the ground. The bowling stint of professionals at both county and club levels naturally evolved into a coaching element. As the years passed, this became more significant. Certainly most clubs had a groundsman whilst the country house pitches also needed expert attention. In this latter category the doubling up of duties was probably more on the gardening front.

As well as masters and alumni coaching cricket at the public schools, the fashion quickly developed of employing resident professional coaches, such as H.H.Stephenson at Uppingham, Tom Emmett at Rugby and James Lillywhite at Marlborough among a string of other highly experienced and gifted players. Several schools had more than one coach and, as the school season began immediately after Easter, often as early as the closing days of March, players who were still active could sometimes find an extra outlet for their talents before the season proper began. As well as Fenner's ground at Cambridge and the Parks at Oxford, it became common for the individual colleges to have cricket grounds. By the 1850s the Oxford colleges hired 25 pros for what was admittedly a shortish season while in 1895 the Cambridge University club took on no less than thirteen paid coaches.[7]

A modicum of paid umpires might also be listed. The convention of an umpire from or on – or if folklore be believed – for each side was a lengthy one reaching back to the earliest of matches. This was coupled with the arbitration of the two gentlemen leading the teams, especially, of course, where money was at stake. That almost natural entitlement of the gentry continued to influence matters on occasion as the system of employing usually retired professionals as umpires in top-class cricket took hold. Occasional stories seep down to us on the friction this sometimes caused. In the 1880s Lord Harris complained to the umpire Robert Thoms about unfair bowling, to which that stalwart fellow replied 'My Lord, we are going to do nothing. It is you gentlemen who have got to do it.' That fairly summed up what, when there was a ticklish issue rather more than the occasional controversial decision, was the ongoing situation. It was down to the authorities to settle, maybe by legislation, a general disputatious matter.[8]

The situation whereby working men sat in condign judgement of their betters is a curio – and it is curious, too, that little has been revealed about how this role change, almost amounting to a mischief night of old when monarchs and jesters exchanged places, operated. Gentlemen may have been used to taking advice from artisan experts like gamekeepers or blacksmiths but not to being ruled by them. It is a tribute to the more mellow mood of the age that it worked tolerably effectively. By this time many amateurs would as schoolboys have become habituated to reacting temperately to coaches and both kinds of cricketer would have been reared in the lesson of the finality of an umpiring decision. The umpires desire to both please their bosses and placate their old comrades possibly neutralised any in-built prejudices and, on the whole, all cricketers appeared to have been reasonably well-conducted. Throwing was the chief cause of discontent. The Australian-born umpire James Phillips created mayhem in the 1890s with his fearless and perhaps over-enthusiastic calling, the culprits including the patrician and irate C.B.Fry. In a complex game such as cricket there has always been a grudging agreement that umpiring errors even themselves out, if not over a match, then over a season. Generally speaking, it would be fair to rank this espousal of the lower class umpire as a tiny piece of evidence of the benign behaviour of the classes then when active in concert.

The story is told of W.G.Grace, not one to suffer fools purporting to be umpires let alone batsmen, bowlers and fielders, gladly, showing disapproval of a contested run out in a match at Birmingham in 1874. Noting this, the Yorkshire umpire Charles (presumably) Webster cried, 'If you had been Jesus Christ I should have given you out.' The Victorian theologian may have wished to add the rider that Jesus Christ would have been unlikely to have shown signs of dissent at his dismissal. That apart, the tale, whether, like many Gracian anecdotes, apocryphal or not, acts as a gentle *resume* of this discussion of the umpire/player class relationship in Victorian cricket.[9]

Professional umpires, players, net bowlers, groundsmen, coaches, some of them part-time, some of them taking two of these tasks – it is difficult to place a correct figure on those making a living, in part or whole, from cricket. It was certainly several thousand with, at the top of a flourishing tree probably 500 in relatively well-paid posts as players and/or coaches in the county, league and prestigious club ranks or attached to schools and colleges. It is logical to surmise that these men learned their trade as members of club teams and it would have been on the basis of club form that they sought professional recognition. While the social profile of some of the elite clubs seems to have remained purely middle class, it must be assumed that the generality of local clubs were giving plenty of chances to young hopefuls from the working classes. Otherwise there would not have been this thriving flow of potential county and league professionals of such good quality. A further assumption might be that in the main they must have come from the upper tiers of that echelon. They would have needed a little bit of brass and a little bit of polish to negotiate the rugged path to success.

Few of them would have been coached at school whereas the blossoming amateur legion benefited from the high-levels of coaching, grounds and fixture-lists of their public schools. Just as many, though by no means all, professional cricketers were born and bred in the upper ranks of their class, an even greater proportion of county amateurs were nursed in the utmost tier of theirs. In the Edwardian period a half of county players were amateurs, overwhelmingly young men from a tight chain of major public schools. Apart from their privileged induction into the game, they also, of course, were the scions of wealthy families who could, for the most part, fund their cricketing activities. Half the county players were drawn from 2% of the population.[10]

The vast network of clubs, with the public schools adding the blue-blooded icing to the fruity cake of ordinary Saturday afternoon endeavour, created a nationwide attachment to cricket. In participation and by following, cricket was, for half a century, the leading national sport, played and enjoyed by all classes.

Good fortune allows us an apposite glimpse about how one cricket club was formed. This was in 1868. Gad's Hill in Kent, where Charles Dickens had settled himself in as country gentleman, was about to start a cricket club. The famous author, who had already showed his interest by having cricket played on his estate, acting as umpire or scorer and entertaining there the nearby Higham cricket club, agreed to be chairman. He contributed £5 for its initial funding and said he would 'overlook its business affairs.' He wrote a three page letter from America to his son Harry about how the club should be organised. It was intended for both 'gentlemen' and 'working men' and his instruction to Harry began 'the first thing to be avoided is, the slightest appearance of patronage....the second thing to be avoided is, the deprival of the men of their just right to manage their own affairs.'

His solution was in itself a little condescending although at the same time ingenious. He commanded Harry to appoint himself as captain so that he could ensure the 'gentlemen' would toe the line with regard to the split membership. Dickens proposed that the gentlemen should pay twice the subscription as the working men but that all should have an equal vote. 'Draw up the club rules (but) whatever you do, let the men ratify; and let them feel their little importance, and at once perceive how much better the business begins to be done.' It is a trifle pious and torturous but it illustrates a progressive essay in bringing fairness and unity to what, basically, was an unjust and divisive situation. The Dickens biographer Peter Ackroyd commented, 'here we have Dickens' dream of society in miniature, an harmonious arrangement of all the classes in which the paternalism of the gentleman captain is linked with the recognition of the 'little importance' of the workers.'[11]

1.   Wray Vamplew *Pay Up and Play the Game; Professional Sport in Britain; 1875-1914* (1988) pp. 51-53.
2.   Sandiford p.55.
3.   Bowen pp. 113-115.
4.   George Orwell in a review of Edmund Blunden's *Cricket Country* in *Manchester Evening News* 20 April 1944. See also Eric Midwinter *Quill on Willow; Cricket in Literature* (2001) chap 3 'The Cricket on the Hearth'.
5.   Brian Bearshaw *From the Stretford End; the Official History of Lancashire County Cricket Club* (1990).
6.   J.R. Webber *The Chronicle of W.G.* (1998).
7.   Sandiford op.cit and Sissons op.cit.
8.   Birley op.cit.
9.   Cited in Midwinter, *Grace* op.cit. p.158.
10. Wynne-Thomas op.cit, p124.
11. Peter Ackroyd *Dickens* (1990) pp. 738/739.

Chapter Six
The Working Class Cricketer

Context is important. The demographics of the middle and working classes and their comparative life-styles paint the canvas against which a cross-class affection for cricket was played out. It was only in the early part of the 19th century that the terms 'middle class' and 'working class', sometimes in the plural, came commonly into use, with categories like 'gentle' and 'simple' now somewhat archaic. Certainly from the ascent to the throne of Queen Victoria in 1837 one may safely deploy the terms without fear of anachronism. It was far from being a caste system. Writing in mid-19th century the perceptive French political scientist, Alexis de Tocqueville suggested that 'the Englishman, unlike the Frenchman, is accustomed to the idea that he can rise in the social scale' and that this was protection against the kind of revolutionary humours of his native land. At the same time, this comforting thought appears to have been pondered upon and accepted as an agreeable situation about which not much further action need be taken. On the whole, there was little urgency to seek to rise in station. There was substantial contentment, perhaps, self-satisfaction, in being in, staying in and knowing one's place.

Lord Palmerston, a leading light of the Whig governments from the late 1840s and prime minster with just a brief interval for ten years 1855 to 1865, understood full well the social model that was emerging and urged it on Britain's more reactionary neighbours: 'we have shown the example as a nation, in which every class of society accepts with cheerfulness the lot which providence has assigned to it; while at the same time every individual of each class is striving to raise himself in the social scale – not by injustice and wrong, not by violence and illegality, but by preserving good conduct, and by the steady and energetic execution of the moral and intellectual faculties with which his creator has endowed him.'[1]

The cricket clubs both of the recreational and the county varieties illustrated the ethic explicit in that statement – and, so as the next chapter will outline, did those who came to watch.

It has some relevance to cricket that the first use of numbers apropos classes was in 1807 when Oxford and Cambridge Universities introduced the concept of first, second and third class degrees, although this was a very rarefied usage given the miniscule sum of persons involved. It was the railways who, in 1838, initiated the usage for popular reference with their first, second and third class carriage system. In 1846 they added the refinement of the hyphen, as in first-class. The second known practice of the 'first class' label was when in the 1840s Fred Lillywhite, that proficient bowler who became equally effective as a chronicler and printer, introduced the branding to grade batsmen. Later bowlers were added and eventually these joint performances led to matches and teams being so judged.[2]

It is a cheering conceit to imagine that Fred Lillywhite, who must have undertaken many train journeys in his career, borrowed the term from the railways, to which national cricket already owed so much. It must be said that the cricket authorities were not so well-organised as the railway companies. The counties and the press argued over the throes of classification for years and it was not until 1894 that a leaden-footed MCC, despairing of the counties' inability to resolve the issue, came to a momentous decision. There was 'no need for further sub-division'. Like, famously, pregnancy, you either were or you weren't. In future there would be first-class teams and matches and, consequently, players – and the rest were not. Like so much of cricket's past – the county championship and Test matches are other instances – this led to sometimes rather frantic efforts by archivists and researchers to ascribe the title retrospectively. This arose partly from the *faux*-religious cult that cricket had become, with a heavy weight of history required as a kind of benediction. But this *ex post facto* approach was in part caused by hapless statisticians faced, a pertinent example, with the risk of W.G.Grace's figures changing grades in 1894. Association football, for instance, was either more fortunate or more neatly managed in that the Football Association was a properly acknowledged national body when it inaugurated for its national club membership the FA Challenge Cup whilst the Football League constructed a well-regulated competition from day one. There was no attempt – there was no need – to latch on earlier activities to the annals as the cricket arbitrators felt obliged to do.

A starting-point in a clearer understanding of the balance of classes must be the numbers involved and here, as on other matters, the historian is lucky in the richness of the data available, much of it contemporary. Dudley Baxter's excellent attempt at social analysis, *National Income*, produced in 1868, estimated that the upper and middle classes constituted between a fifth and a quarter of the population. He calculated that the population of England and Wales was 21m – the census returns for 1861 and 1871 show 20m and 22.7m respectively, so he was clearly close in his arithmetic. Of these he reckoned there were some 4.8m in the top and about 16.1m in the bottom of the two broad bands. This rough split of 20/80 to 25/75 middle class/working class is still an approximate ratio that acts as a guide for general social study, changing slightly to 30/70 during the early decades of the 20th century.[3]

The spur to a rising and more influential middle class was patently the burgeoning place of commerce and industry in the economy, but such growth brought with it other demands. Urbanisation and the necessary and allied provision of public services boosted the strength of the professions, among them doctors, lawyers, teachers, engineers and public servants of all kinds. The number in the 'public service and professional sector' in 1851 was 200,000. In 1891 it was 560,000 and there were similar rises in the ranks of the other professional cadres.

Contemporary scholars noted a distinction as between the lower and upper middle classes. The lower sector class segment was formally recognised in the 1850s; having identified that nether section, then, perforce, there had to be a corresponding higher group. This division was made necessary because of a surprisingly wide spectrum of income. What was even more amazing was the numerical differential. The middle classes had grown enormously because of the prodigious call in a dominantly urban and mercantile economy for what would later be called white collar workers such as clerks. 2m of the roughly 4.8m in the middle classes were actually earners, the rest being mainly wives, children and other dependents. Of these 2m only 200,000 could be described as 'upper', leaving the huge majority of 1.8m in the 'lower' bracket. In brief, the former earned £300 annually or more rising to an affluent 7500 men with over £5000. The latter, who came on the continent to be described as the *petit bourgeoisie* were composed almost equally between those whose income was £100 to £300 and those who earned less than £100.

The flood of members into the bottom columns of the middle classes goes some way to explaining the comparative easiness of class relationships in Victorian Britain. The novels of Charles Dickens are awash with a stream of such underpaid minions, legal and accounting clerks scratching away at ledgers on high stools in musty offices: Newman Noggs, Tim Linkinwater, Mr Wemmick, Mr Flintwich, Mr Guppy...the roster is endless – and we even know that Bob Crachitt's pre-redemption income was 15s a week.

On what the Americans would call the other side of the tracks, there were in 1867 close on 8 million manual workers. Their range of wages was from 12s (60p) a week (£30 a year) for the unskilled to 35s (£1.75p) a week (£88 a year) for the million strong band of skilled workers. During the preceding twenty years wages in the United Kingdom had jumped in real terms by 32%. For purposes of real-life comparison, the weekly wage for sample trades was soldiers, 12s; farm workers, 14s; railwaymen, postmen, miners and textile workers, 21/23s; blacksmiths and, perhaps surprisingly, seamen, 25s, and the aristocrats of the working classes, engine drivers and skilled building artisans, 35s.

As regularised county cricket became established in the last decades of the 19th century, the basic cricketer's weekly wage was comprised of a guaranteed ground staff payment of £2 or £3 plus a winter retainer of 10s or £1. This was fleshed out with appearance money of usually £5 for a home and £6 for an away fixture, with the possibility a win bonus, normally £1. Talent money, occasional collections and, with ten years obedient service the common criterion, a possible benefit match were additional to this. This complex scale produced a wide differential, ranging from 30s to £8 a week, as averaged over a year. An aspect of the differential was, of course, the gap between the richer and poorer counties. As a rare extra, there was £10 for representative games, such as Test or Gentlemen and Players matches.[4]

There were two counterweights to these superficially attractive figures. On the one side, the season lasted only 22 weeks and the search for winter work could be difficult, particularly as the economy became evermore factory-based and the old-time piece work in cottage industries that had stood the veteran pros in good stead decayed. On the other side, the cricketers had to pay for their own kit and equipment and also the costs of accommodation and meals. These first-class cricketers also had to buy their own third-class railway tickets for away matches. Most tradesmen then had to buy and maintain the tools of their craft, which most of them did with affectionate care, but the factory system, whether based on mill, mine or foundry, was normally community-centred; the majority of workers walked to work.

Taking a pot-shot at an individual case, one might estimate that a regular first eleven player, appearing in most games for a relatively well-to-do county team would earn £3 to £4 a week over a full year. Even with the burden of away match costs, but bearing in mind the possibility of winter work, this compares favourably with not only the top layer of the working class but also the bottom layer of the middle class.

Professional cricketers in this regard were, therefore, among those working class men who through force of circumstance enjoyed similar life-styles with the million or so middle-class men with annual salaries of around £100 more or less. Especially in the cities, where first-class cricket was chiefly played, they must have rented the same type of accommodation, made their purchases in the same type of shops, had their children attending the same type of school, led their families in attendance at the same type of church, encountered one another on the same type of family walks, and so on.

What remained constant was that the working man in this situation was sat proudly on top of his world while the middle class gentleman felt humbled and disconsolate at the bottom of his social ladder. They were worse off in that they had to keep up appearances. *The Diary of a Nobody*, the classic account of lower middle class social humiliations and foiled ambitions, conveys this sensibility admirably. Written by George and illustrated by his brother Weedon Grossmith, it was published in 1892 after serialisation in *Punch*, with Mr Charles Pooter, a sedate City of London clerk, residing at the Laurels, Brickfield Terrace, Holloway, the diffident diarist.

Nonetheless, this overlap of class income helped build the arch that bridged the gap between the classes and contributed to the comparative lack of social acrimony at this time. In that the amateur cricketer came from the higher echelons of middle and upper class background, this did not apply so aptly to the actual alliance of professionals and gentlemen in cricketing play. In fact, the players must also have been wryly aware that many of the gentlemen were better remunerated than themselves. With plentiful expenses and bogus posts like assistant secretary, the counties contrived to uphold a scandalous Shamateur regime for a hundred years.

It was all the result of the tension between an adoration of sporting ethics and a yearning for sporting success. The authorities blinkered their eyes. The main recipients are now well-attested, with W.G.Grace, by today's reckoning comfortably in receipt of over £1m from his cricketing activities. Other celebrity Shamateurs included Surrey's W.W.Read, with £150 a year for a sinecure secretaryship, expenses of £4 a game, an annual bonus of £100 and a season ticket to and from the Oval. Archie MacLaren is another whose trail of payments for a number of spurious reasons is colourful and lengthy while stars like A.E.Stoddart and Gilbert Jessop have also come under this clouded spotlight. The anonymous journalist-cricketer – Pelham Warner referred to himself as 'Mr Warner' when reporting his own cricketing exploits in the press – was another bending of the ethics. MCC did hold an enquiry in 1879 into 'the definition and qualification of amateur cricketers'. £50 was decreed as the maximum expenses for a season; at the turn of the century the amateur expenses for a Test match were 30s a day plus first-class train fare and hospitality. There were professionals at £4 a game who counted themselves lucky to earn £50 each summer.

One might interpose here a word on the income of the league professional. In the pre-World War I days it was not princely. The top Lancashire league pros might have received £4 a match, a total of about £80 for the summer but in more lowly clubs it was as poor as £2, usually with the proviso that ground-keeping and coaching were part of the deal. Collections occasionally added a pound or two, rarely more, to the earnings. Patently, it was not a full-time job.[5] The stirring tale of Sydney Barnes, world class bowler as he was, is an exceptional one. Independent-minded, stubborn and mentally extremely astute, he negotiated his way through Test, county and league cricket with unerring skill and judgement. A high point of his steadfast career was when the Church club paid him £8 a week plus performance bonuses and collections. With something like £250 for a summer's work, he was probably earning more than the amateur and, as he was a diligent clerk and talented calligrapher, he found both winter and post-career jobs with reasonable pay. He might be said to have eventually crossed that magical line between the player and the gentleman.

If the professional cricketers were a little ahead economically of their class, the real downside was the shortness of the career. The news was not all bad. The complexities of and interest in cricket were such that, as has already been mentioned, there was a host of post-playing jobs for cricketers, ranging from scorers to bat and ball makers. From a mixture of sources, one might hazard the guess that upwards of two-third of pros found some cricket associated work when retired from playing. Publicans were probably the next highest occupational choice.[6] Professional footballers were less fortunate in that as in other respects. The benefit system helped, as long as the weather held, and the Cricketers' Fund Friendly Society, established in 1857 by the old-style Exhibition pros, also assisted admirably. It existed until well after World War II but its genuine identity was in that former age when about the time the CFFS was founded the Friendly Society movement was at its strongest. However, in that pension-less era, the later lives of professional cricketers thus paint an extraordinary picture of extremes. Poverty, illness, premature death, alcoholism and suicide were at one end of the gamut and highly successful business enterprise at the other.

While some, like John Wisden or William Gunn, profitably developed major sport equipment businesses – who among the *aficionados* didn't want a copy of 'the Cricketer's Bible' or a Gunn and Moore cricket bat? - whereas Archie MacLaren, while majestically regal as a batsman, was more of a court jester when it came to the umpteen business enterprises of which he made a pig's ear. On his death William Gunn left £54,392. Yet John Jackson, having risen from poor origins to become a feared quick bowler, declined into impoverishment and died a pauper in 1901 in Liverpool workhouse infirmary. (Not quite so miserable an ending as one might fear; by 1901 the poor law hospitals, like Manchester's Crumpsall and Withington, were among the country's leading such institutions, well-disciplined and pioneering, having rid themselves of much of the Dickensian gloom and horror.) Two great professional cricketers, Arthur Shrewsbury and Albert Trott shot themselves, or rather himself; but so did A.E.Stoddart, an outstanding amateur batsman, sustaining a grim cricketing parade of *felo de se* which David Frith has chronicled with diligent and perceptive acuity.[7]

In short, between these diverse points were also many who, by the norms of the time for a working class man, lived moderately well.

This was in part because of the *noblesse oblige* influence of one or two potentates of the game such as Lord Hawke of Yorkshire and Lord Harris of Kent, both of whom, if with more than a whiff of condescension, insisted on reasonable treatment for professionals. The former, faced as captain with a Yorkshire team he famously described as ten drunks and a parson, strove to smarten up and discipline his almost wholly inebriated and only slightly Christian troupe. With such accoutrements as the county cap, he enjoyed some success in his aims while Lord Harris said in 1886 that so progressive were his views that some claimed he was 'a cricket socialist'. It is unlikely that Keir Hardie, let alone Karl Marx, would have spotted in Lord Harris a fellow searcher for the Red Dawn – and they would have been right. But both Lord Hawke and he demanded respect and they were prepared to tender the same in return.

Like so much of the Victorian social equation the significant factor was respectability. If the working man toed the line in dignified fashion and kicked not against the pricks of the ongoing order, then he would be treated decently and fairly. Dutiful behaviour was at the heart of the relationship. Complaining, quibbling and defiance were not. Let us be quite fair to Lord Harris and Lord Hawke and others of their ilk, among them A.N.Hornby and on his more thoughtful days W.G.Grace, they were ready to respond positively. There were others perhaps who expected the deference as a right and took it off-handedly for granted.

As county cricket waxed and Exhibition cricket waned, the professional became the subject of more intensive control than hitherto, his reaction to this a measure of his respectability. Voices sympathetic to the pros have tended to view the change as exploitative, the hearty entrepreneurial buccaneers replaced by galley-slave drudges. There is no doubt that the county system was more controlling than that of the Exhibition teams but to imagine that any group overseen by the likes of William Clarke or W.G.Grace, autocrats both, mirrored the ideals of the Rochdale Co-operative Pioneers would be wide of the mark. Although slow to reach tidy solutions in terms of how the championship was arranged, the county schedule was competitive and thus some refinement of player flexibility was demanded. A further point to note is the size of the cadre. Of its nature the Exhibition XIs in any one season could only offer opportunities to 40 or so players while the counties offered work to four or five times as many; it is a tricky ethical conundrum whether a few freer men in work beats many men doing the same job is more restrictive conditions.

The defining year was in 1873. The decision was agreed that no player should play for more than one county in a season. Roger Iddison, for example, had contrived to play for both Lancashire and Yorkshire in the same summer during the 1860s. That was tantamount to being recruited by both sides in the contemporaneous conflict of the American Civil War. There was a reasonableness about the edict. Moreover, a deep sense of loyalty, fostered in school, regiment and elsewhere, led the authorities to expect such devotion among their inferiors; the professional flitting hither and yon lacked patriotic backbone. But the devil was in the detail, for a player had to opt by birth or residence of two years for a particular county and that was very limiting. It applied to amateurs but never seems to have been so strictly applied with the 'occasional residence', such as a parental home, clause benefiting the more geographically advantaged middle and upper classes.

Moving freely each summer would have been workable, even legitimate but this birth and residential rider was stultifying. Pity the poor young professional born or living in a shire which could afford few if any professionals or his counterpart in a well-provided county who, falling short of the high standard required there, could not easily try his arm elsewhere. A player wishing or ordered to move was faced with a two year denial of top-class cricket as he established residence in another county, even if he could find one ready with a promise of fuller employment three seasons ahead. The convention of a benefit after ten years of cricketing application with good conduct was another tether. While gradually slackened in rigidity, the residential rule endured a hundred years. Tom Graveney played no county cricket in 1961 as he made what in terms of time was a lengthy journey from Gloucestershire to neighbouring Worcestershire.

Many generations of cricket-lovers grew up enjoying the romantic fancy that the county was represented by county-born or bred players. There is no doubt that the county then had a profounder identity - 'county commonwealths' as Lewis Namier the great historian of Hanoverian Britain called them – with county as important to some as national birthright. Football and cricket crowds still revel in the local boy making good although, truth to tell, they delight the more in supporting a winning team. Yorkshire, with its broad acres and multitude of cricket clubs, and in spite of Lord Hawke having been born in Lincolnshire, took the blood-cult very seriously until recent times. It is with sorrow that one discovers the pastoral idyll of the home-spun team was, not least at a time when the county championship was still some years away from being a properly regulated and orthodox competition, no more than a blatant piece of class legislation.

It was an act in restraint of trade that was not seriously challenged until the Packer era while only latterly have counties been forced to agree more binding and player-friendly annual contracts to stop their staffs being recruited for winter cricket without their permission. At the time, of course, it was viewed rather differently. The abiding concept was the master and servant relationship. Equity had no part in that. Britons might never, never be slaves but even freemen had to work and eat, and their employers – mill owner, farmer, stately home, county cricket club – held the aces. Trades unionism, while on the rise, was still in its infancy as a negotiating mechanism. Cricketers, like farm labourers, were spread widely in penny numbers, not solidly together in sizable mining or textile communities. The only two attempts at what it is probably ostentatious to label strike action – seven Notts professionals in 1881 and five England players in 1896 – were both met with ruthless firmness. In other words, professional cricketers were no better and no worse off than their *compadres* in the upper levels of the working class.

Another contextual lens is the manner in which other sports dealt with the class riddle. Plainly, the poser only arose where participants required paid help or spectatorship necessitated it. There is little data for anyone interested in writing a thesis on croquet, lacrosse or hockey professionalism at this time. Golf approaches cricket in that it developed the club professional who often doubled as ground keeper and teacher or maybe trebled as a club and ball maker. The British Open Championship, open, that is, to professionals and amateurs, dates from 1861 and that has safely sailed through the years without undue tumult. The professionals Willie Park and the Toms Morris, father and son were the early winners. They would not, of course, have been allowed in the clubhouse. Popular although golf was in parts of Scotland, the English boom came late in the 19th century. In 1880 there was a sorry total of twelve courses in England; by 1914 it was over a thousand, providing wholesome employment for a large work-force.

This was the era of a huge expansion in British sport and a time when the formation of national ruling bodies and league, championship and allied competitive structures was intensified.[8] The mature staples of horse racing and boxing, both dominated by professional performers, continued. Horse racing remained perhaps the most popular of games despite the growth of cricket and its rewards for high-class jockeys were mouth-watering. The legendary Fred Archer, champion jockey in thirteen years up to 1886, shot himself - shadows of Arthur Shrewsbury and Albert Trott – in that year aged 29. He left over £66,000.

The *credo* of Athleticism was purest and some would add nastiest in, aptly enough, athletics and also in rowing. The Amateur Athletic Association formed in 1880 laid down stringent requirements. It defined the amateur in social as well as economic terms with its offer of membership to 'any gentleman' who eschewed payments and was not 'a mechanic, artisan or labourer.' Rowing purged the sport of any professionalism, even including coaching. Separate clubs emerged for gentlemen, tradesmen and 'watermen', who were those boatmen doing it for a living.

The football codes, like cricket, were faced with professionalism. The Football Association, founded in 1863, accepted that legitimate expenses might be paid but otherwise stood firm. In 1885 it was reluctantly decided that, with certain restrictions, wages would be allowed. The authorities rightly thought this compromise was preferable to what Charles Alcock, Secretary of the FA and a power also in the cricket world, called 'veiled professionalism'. Although the dodge of pushing a few shillings in the football boot was never eradicated, in the main this division into a professional spectator and an amateur recreational sport proved to be effective. There were oddities. In 1885 J.H.Forrest, of Blackburn Rovers, became England's first professional international player; playing his first game against Scotland he had to wear a blue jersey to distinguish him from his white-shirted unpaid team-mates. With the establishment of the Football League in 1888 the professional game became increasingly serious. Registration was introduced which was in some ways harsher than the cricketer's bond; once registered, a player was more or less tied willy-nilly to a club with the possibility of being sold by transfer to another team.

The Rugby Union, formed by the breakaway of clubs from the FA in 1871, suffered its own fissure in 1895 over the question of 'broken time' payments, that is expenses paid to players who had lost earnings because of playing. The RU was adamantly opposed to this practice which led to the formation of the Northern Rugby Union, later the Rugby League. By 1910 there were about 400 Rugby League professionals while, after a latish start, a sudden surge had brought the number of full- or part-time paid footballers to 5000. A rough estimate would be that there were about 8000 or 9000 professional sportsmen in the UK by the end of the Edwardian period where there had been but a handful sixty years before.

There were one or two gentlemen who opted for professional status; Surrey's George Lohmann was the son of a Stock Exchange employee and the father of Lancashire's Arthur Paul was a senior army offcier, later Chief Constable of the Isle of Man. One or two played as amateurs and then turned professional, among them W.G.Grace's cousin Walter Gilbert of Middlesex and Edwin Diver of Surrey. It was a tiny band. The stigma was quite toxic. Being a gentleman in Victorian England, with all its subtle gradations and mannerisms, was to occupy a very particular status. W.G.Grace is but the most well-known of those who found it impossible to choose between being a pure 'gentleman' and an openly remunerated 'player'.

Nonetheless, cricket by accident or design managed the cohesion of the classes with more fluidity than any other sport where professionalism had become an essential factor. The County Cricket team was a microcosm of what was evolving in many domains of cultural and social experience in late 19th and early 20th century. Its arithmetic was surprisingly close to the norm in its proportions. As the 20th century dawned and for a further generation, the average county side would have two or three amateurs and eight or nine professionals. This very tidily represented the 25%/75% of that large central mass of the then British population which comprised the aspiring working and the earnest middle classes.

All in all, and for all the snobbery and hypocrisy involved, cricket's essay in class alliance offered during this period perhaps the least objectionable sporting model in a class-obsessed society.

1. Richard J. Evans *The Pursuit of Power; Europe 1815-1914* (2016) pp 225/228
2. Wynne-Thomas p.81
3. Eric Midwinter *The Collective Age 1850-1950;the Rise and Fall of a Fairer Society* (2017) The following discussion of social class statistics leans heavily on chapter 3 'Collectivism and Social Structure'
4. Sissons op.cit p.85ff and passim.
5. Sandiford op.cit. Pp 86/87
6. Sissons op.cit. Especially pp 140/143
7. David Frith *By Their Own Hand; a Study of Cricket's Suicides* (1990) and *Silence of the Heart; Cricket's Suicides* (2001)
8. Judith Flanders *Consuming Passions; Leisure and Pleasure in Victorian Britain* (2006) fascinating in general but in particular for this topic chapter 11 'Sporting Life' pp.419/465. For a simple list of the dates of this 'bureaucratisation' of all games, see Eric Midwinter *Fair Game; Myth and Reality in Modern Sport* (1986) p.54/56

Chapter Seven
The Cricket Crowd

The crowd came as a bit of a surprise to the cricketing authorities. Grounds had been enclosed more to repel than embrace the common horde. Lord's had imposed charges to deter the bothersome element and, as William Clarke and other ground entrepreneurs discovered, over a hundred years period prior to the 1860s, much as the lower orders enjoyed cricket, they preferred it gratis. These were clubs and remained so. By that token they were the province of subscribing members, initially playing members, soon joined by non-playing members who enjoyed watching. One or two counties were more watcher than player orientated in their origins but, in the outcome, they all, along with MCC, adopted some form of two-tier membership, three-tier if one counts the usual provision made at lower cost for the ladies and children of members.

A taste for spectating had been renewed by the Exhibition XIs although it would appear that some of their matches had been, in part or whole, of the typical Georgian mould, whereby an entrepreneur, ordinarily a publican, gathered together as many as wished to attend, hopeful that their consumption of his wares would leave him with a profit. Gradually, a combine of increased leisure and improved pay coupled with the burgeoning interest in cricket produced large and regular attendances. To this should be added the spiralling interest of the press, both the specialist sporting magazines and the daily or weekly newspapers. Much cheaper newspapers and a widened literacy boosted the daily reading about cricket in all classes of society.[1]

Almost the only signs of misconduct at cricket grounds in this more quiescent epoch were when the new wine of milling crowds clashed with the old bottle of inadequate grounds. Unruliness at the Eton and Harrow fixtures at Lord's in 1863 and 1873 was caused by overcrowding. In 1864 MCC invited the Metropolitan Police to extend the long arm of the law but lack of space and amenities were the real problems. 40,000 attended the two days of the 1873 game, 27,000 of them paying, 13,000 members and guests. MCC next played the old card of raising the admission from 1s to 2s 6d. Paying customers dropped to 15,000, still making an overfull arena.

Some idea of the antiquated nature of the Lord's ground is explicit in the 1864 announcement of increased prices at the schools' match. These were 1s for those 'on foot'; on horseback 2s6d; two wheeled carriages 5s and the four wheeled type 10s. In 1861 700 carriages had paraded at Lord's for the first day of the Eton and Harrow encounter; in 1876 there were 1200 carriages. Strangely, the Eton and Harrow match stretched the Lord's resources more than most games and was one of the motivators of modernisation. It joined Royal Ascot and the Henley Regatta among the major events of the season. One had to be there. The Varsity match also commanded large crowds; in 1892 52,000 paid for admission over the three days, with a large contingent of members and guests in addition

Like those other posh affairs, these two prestigious fixtures attracted a gaping throng as intrigued by the passing show of the rich and famous as fascinated by horses, boats and youthful cricketers. The Old Harrovian John Galsworthy chose the Eton and Harrow match for one of the most compelling scenes in *The Man of Property* the first volume of his *The Forsyte Saga* (1906). The seriously introverted Soames Forsyte sees his 'property', the beautiful but to him icily cold Irene among 'six thousand top hats, four thousand parasols', she the cynosure of charmed attention, he the depressed, tight-lipped, silently bitter loner.

It is highly relevant to mention hereabouts another well-received item on the Lord's menu – the annual Gentlemen and Players fixture. Sides had been cobbled together called 'the Gentlemen of England' for occasional games but it was in 1806, with cricket in its doldrums, that the gentlemen first tried their hand against the professionals. They did so with abject results. After a couple such games in that year, there was no further encounter until 1819. When fixtures were organised they tended, such was the frailty of unpractised gentlemen against skilled craftsmen, to be one-sided. Handicaps were occasionally used, such as eighteen gents, the pros having to bat in front of larger wickets or even that old stand-by of the clubs, the actual inclusion of a professional bowler or two. Parity came – and with it a boom time in attendances – when W.G.Grace and a flow of well-instructed and experienced amateurs arrived on the cricketing scene.

Old Trafford, like the two London venues, was also thrown off guard by the sudden surge of interest in cricket in general and W.G.Grace in particular. On his first visit to Old Trafford in 1878 between 15,000 and 20,000 flocked into the ground on the Saturday in such profusion that they strayed on to the pitch and shortened the boundaries. It is perhaps artless to imagine that Billy Midwinter's presence in the Gloucestershire team might have added a few to the gate. The Oval, too, was discomfited, for instance, on the first Monday of September 1880 when there was an 'unprecedented attendance' of over 20,000 to watch the Australians.

The fame of W.G.Grace and the Australians was to fill and indeed overfill many cricket grounds and bring about vast improvements. The horses and carriages vanished from Lord's where gradual reconstruction led by the end of the century to a ground capable of welcoming 30,000 patrons in reasonable comfort, By that same point the Oval could accommodate 25,000, Old Trafford the better part of 20,000 and Trent Bridge 15,000 while the three main Yorkshire venues of Headingley, Bramall Lane and Bradford Park Avenue could each hold 20,000 or more.

Throughout the country at county and club level there was a rash of building projects, with pavilions, stands, scoreboards, press boxes and all mod cons for the milling crowds. Turnstiles, in effect mechanical updates of the swivel stiles of animal husbandry, were introduced in the early 1870s. The 2000 or 3000 daily totals of the 1840s were, on occasion, as much as ten times that by the end of the Victorian era. The gradient has been delineated as, in respect of daily average attendances, 3000 in the 1840s; 4000 in the 1860s; 8000 in the 1880s and 10,000 in the 1900s, with by this stage 15,000 or 20,000 not uncommon. The county record for the 19th century was set in 1892 at the Oval when over the three days of the Surrey and Nottinghamshire game, then one of the choicest fixtures of the summer, 63,763 people paid; it has been estimated that with members and guests over 100,000 watched that match. For the Lord's Test of 1886 over 33,000 shimmied through the new turnstiles whilst at Leicestershire's Grace Road in 1878 the visiting Australian tourists attracted an attendance record of 12,000.[2]

Another source[3] suggests the following average daily paid numbers (that is, exclusive of members) at the beginning of the 20th century: 4500 for Sussex; 7000 for Essex; 8000 for Middlesex; 12,000 for Surrey and 17,000 for Yorkshire, Thus although the London based clubs and those centred in major industrial conurbations obviously attracted the largest custom, all the sixteen counties that competed for the County Championship at the turn of the century were reasonably supported. As well as the demographic disparity, there were, of course, the vagaries of the climate and the variables of team performance to take into account but all the counties were being supported in some degree. It has been calculated that average county attendances per day ranged from 8000 to 24,000, inclusive of both members and ordinary paying customers. In 1900 there were 209 first-class games played in the British Isles. Very roughly, including both paying and subscribing patrons, 1.5m people attended those matches.

With the possible exception of horse racing, cricket had been the most popular sport up to and at that time. Many local clubs also had healthy followings. Some northern league clubs had regular gates of 6000 and the more prestigious southern clubs often enjoyed a similar patronage. The first FA Challenge Cup Final was played at the Oval in 1872 before a scattering of 2000 supporters on a ground where 20,000 for a day's county cricket was not exceptional. Cricket was inexpensive. 6d was the standard charge everywhere, even Lord's, for a day's outing, 1s was the charge for a Test match, often for a game in which W.G.Grace was starring, for some of the festival matches and, out of sync with the rest, Surrey's fixtures at the Oval. League cricket was 2d and 4d. Football League prices were slightly higher at 3d and 6d. At many cricket matches ladies were admitted free.

Although the Oxford and Cambridge and the Eton and Harrow meetings attracted an elitist following of loyal *alumni* and their families, it is apparent that, even on those occasions when the lower orders came to rubberneck, there was something of a social mix, while across the range of county, league and recreational cricket the audiences must have had a modicum if not a majority of working class representatives. There has been a tendency to think that the great London cricket crowds were very much more middle class than their counterpart in the major industrial cities. While this may have been marginally true, there may have been some of the 'snooty London – sooty Leeds' sentiment about this contention. Despite the prominence of the textile, mining and other heavily industrialised trades in the remarkable growth of industry in Britain, the metropolis also had its own industrial revolution. The population of Greater London shot astronomically from 1.4m at the beginning to just over 7m at the end of the 19th century. It had a huge proletariat, the diversity of its occupations blurring the vision of the historian habituated to observing the industrial work-force in blocs of miners or cotton operatives. As befitted a capital city, London's industries tended toward such work as the docks, the building and construction trades, the food and clothing manufactures, armaments and the like. There is every reason to believe that a dedicated minority of these workers would have wended their way to London's cricket venues, especially perhaps the Oval. Cricket crowds were generally representative of the class breakdown in society at large.

The lay-out of the larger modernised grounds illustrates this. The convention was adopted of a pavilion, sometimes with winged extra stands, for members and guests, with the remainder of the circle taken up by 'free seats' or other terracing, rows of benches and grassed mounds.

The inference to be drawn is that, on average, a quarter of the crowd were members in the pavilion and its surrounds, all of them, as of right, drawn from the middle classes and well able to afford the one or two guineas fee. The stands flanking the pavilion might also have included specially priced accommodation for non-member gentlemen and perhaps their families. Ladies' pavilions were not unknown. The other three quarters of the circuit of seating and on many smaller grounds grassy knolls for standing or sitting were for the working class spectators, obviously in goodly numbers. However, the overlap of income of poorer middle class and better off working class earners must be recalled, so that there must have been some mixing of the respectable artisan and the underpaid clerk, for example, all of it illustrative of the enforced closeness of the two main classes at their income-based boundaries.

The standard football ground, given its rectangular shape, is a neater example of the principle. Contrary to popular belief, professional football was not an entirely plebeian pursuit. While not as blessed with the encouragement of peers and knights of the realm as was cricket, there was a lot of interest and, of course, investment, by local businessmen and a keen awareness that a successful team was good for the community and its economy. The usual construct was a stand of, paradoxically, seats for this class, most frequently behind one touchline and with dressing rooms and offices often based thereunder, with the working class standing on the sets of terraces, one opposite the grandstand and one behind each goal. The demographic arithmetic was flawless; 25% middle and 75% working class.

In this later Victorian period and up until the First World War, one must recollect that the combined total of an aspiring and respectable working class and a serious-minded and hard-working middle class was, a conservative estimate, well over 80% of the population, that is all but the poorer, unskilled sub-class and the upper class. Alike in mind-set, religious outlook, moral code and domestic habit, they constituted a formidable coalition.

The cricketing alliance, whether at participation or spectating level, was not some exotic novelty. A deeper understanding of what at first sight appears to be a divisive process, with amateurs and professionals using separate dressing rooms, entrances to the pitch, overnight accommodation, travel facilities and so forth, comes with a grasp of the widespread manifestation of the phenomenon.

The strategy of sharing the same experience from class standpoints was not new. What was novel was the concentrated incidence of this joint happening. The theatre had long practised this and continued to do so. Indeed, even the music hall, long believed to be the haunt of the working class, has been shown to have enjoyed, especially when big business adopted it and sought respectability for the product, a considerable middle-class custom. The church practice of the free pew and the pew paid for is another example, as is, at the other end of the ethical gamut, the pub with, increasingly, a saloon and a public bar.

A cheery example is the seaside holiday resort. The advent of the week's holiday for many workers, with, eventually, pay included, brought thousands usually by rail to the beaches and promenades. By 1911 there were 145 registered seaside resorts around the British coast. The brash leader was Blackpool which welcomed 1.5m boarders and 3m day visitors every year. It is a particularly apt example, for, of course, many seaside towns hosted first-class cricket among the attractions on offer. The Sussex county ground at Hove and the deployment of Scarborough and Hastings for late season festival weeks are the obvious instances but Blackpool, no less, as well as Southport and Lytham St Annes, along with Clacton, Bournemouth, Southend and others might be listed.

Consciously or otherwise, many seaside resorts developed a select and a less select end or, as in the case of Blackpool, two select wings and a working class centre. One could opt for different styles of accommodation according to income and taste – and then stroll down the same promenades, walk down the same piers, watch the same minstrel or pierrot shows, listen to the same brass bands – Britain had 50,000 brass bands in 1900 – and cluster in the same pier pavilions and promenade shelters when the same inevitable rain fell.

The trains that carried the holdiay-makers to and from the resorts were overt in their retailing, using the first, second and third class nomenclature unashamedly. Interestingly, it was in 1875, as the new social order was beginning to peak, that the railway companies upgraded the third and abolished the second class carriages, so that they basically ran trains with working and middle-class compartments, conveying professional and amateur cricketers in each respectively.

Another example is that of Britain's first venture into the light music industry with the extremely business-like Gilbert and Sullivan operas. In concert with the entrepreneur Richard D'Oyly Carte, Gilbert and Sullivan took the theatrical world by storm. By the time of the composer's death in 1900 there had been 6000 G&S performances in London and 30,000 in the provinces, there were 3000 amateur licences sold a year and there was a vast outcrop of sheet music, band parts, souvenirs, gifts and the like. From 'parlour' ballads sung domestically and mock-madrigals for choirs to barrel-organs, military bands and whistling errand boys, the melodic strains were ubiquitous. Those holiday-makers, middle-class or working class, pausing by the band on the prom at Eastbourne or Skegness, would have bent their ears to a selection of tunes from *Pirates of Penzance*. Spectators, whether of high or low birth, at Scarborough or Hastings cricket grounds would have been entertained by the brass band playing a medley of *HMS Pinafore* music.

As an exercise in the shrewd salesmanship of light music, it was not emulated until Beatlemania generations later but what is striking is the keen awareness of W.S.Gilbert of the cross-class potential. Over and again he used culinary metaphors to describe this. He searched for what he called 'the gastronomic mean', musical theatre that would 'supply a meal of one dish at which all the community are to sit down.' 'Tripe and onions' would be found tasty in the pit but not the stalls; *vice versa* 'sweetbread and truffles'. So Gilbert argued that 'a plain leg of mutton and boiled potatoes is the most stable fare of all.' On another foray into the kitchen for inspiration, he claimed to provide 'rump steak and oyster sauce for all.'

Another who had a clear-eyed understanding of the 'integrated culture' of these two staple classes was Gilbert's own Guru, Charles Dickens. While accepting, even approving, the strict class divide *per se*, he preached the benevolent creed of *entente cordiale* between the classes as the foundation for social harmony, as we have already noted in respect of Gad's Hill cricket club.. 'We are all fellow-travellers to the same grave,' he wrote in *A Christmas Carol*, 'and not a race of different creatures bound on other journeys.'

His influence was enormous, first among equals in the prosperous book and publications industry. During Queen Victoria's reign the numbers in the printing and stationery trades doubled to 200,000 and the number of books published annually rose from 2000 to 10,000. There were 42,000 Victorian novels written by 1500 novelists; a hundred of them each had one hundred titles published. They were chiefly family novels but they were also often and always in Dickens' case, read by all social classes. They contrived to be both classic and popular, much more than today. A fine example of Dickensian social concord and his wish that the classes should be joined in 'fusion...on a good, common, mutual ground' is to be found in his master-servant studies. Some are, to be sure, acrimonious, exemplifying how unfruitful such relationships might be but others are, as in the splendid illustration of Mr Pickwick and Sam Weller, portrayals of wholesome and reciprocal affection, images of what has been called 'the democracy of laughter.' One might imagine Mr Pickwick and Sam as fellow-members of the Gad's Hill CC XI.

Charles Dickens employed the vogue device of cross-class romance, as in the poignant tales of Pip and Estella in *Great Expectations,* itself a telling analysis of the difficulties of changing from working man to gentleman. or Eugene Wrayburn and Lizzie Hexam in *Our Mutual Friend.* Every mainline pantomime – Cinderella and Prince Charming; Aladdin and Princess Balroubadour; Dick Whittington and Alice Fitzwarren – represents this trope. Gilbert followed suit – the G&S comic operas have been termed, not altogether kindly, 'intelligent pantomime' – in almost every libretto, with, for instance, Frederic and Mabel in *The Pirates of Penzance* or Ralph Rackstraw and Josephine in *HMS Pinafore.* The Victorian public avidly read and eagerly watched cross-class stories. Everyone had characters with whom they could socially identify.

The social and cultural concordance enjoyed by the classes and its celebration in their literature and theatre was of the utmost importance to the watching of cricket and indeed other sports. The older inhabitants of later Victorian Britain must have marvelled at the changed outlook on the teeming host compared with in their younger days. In a phrase, the crowd was no longer feared.

Memories of the Luddite riots, the 'Captain Swing' agricultural unrest and the hard-line militancy of a minority in the Chartist agitation had not faded yet, but surprisingly and suddenly, it was deemed legitimate for vast assemblages to forgather regularly, in fact, during the cricket season almost every day, often with little or no policing.

The Great Exhibition of 1851 was a test-case and marked a step-change in the authorities' view of the English crowd. 6m people, notionally almost a quarter of the population, visited the splendours of the Crystal Palace, on an average of 43,000 daily. Bear in mind, too, that this was more an educative exercise than any sort of funfair and yet train loads of working men and their families were motivated to make the trip, frequently with paternalistic bosses underwriting the costs and making the arrangements for travel and accommodation.

It is a matter of prurient interest that it was at the Great Exhibition that the first penny-in-the-slot toilets were made available; 800,000 men, women and children of all classes, took advantage of the amenity. Before this just a few 'chalets de convenience' had been supplied for the gentry on ceremonious occasions, the use of French itself pointing to a cloying inhibition about such matters, although soon 'public conveniences' were being built by local authorities. Now cricket ground administrators, along with the owners and managers of other arenas, were having, in the face of much larger audiences, to take this issue into account and provide facilities, even if 'spending a penny' had to be embraced as yet another prudish euphemism.

Behaviour at the Great Exhibition was exemplary. The old Duke of Wellington, but a few months of his life remaining, but, as ever, sniffing the air for the rank odour of rebelliousness, had been horrified at the thought of thousands upon thousands of workaday folk heading for Hyde Park. His strong advice had been to place no less than 15,000 troops on hand to crush incipient revolt. He could not have made a wilder prophecy. Calm reigned. The Duke did, however, make one winning contribution on a topic which again touched on the unspoken subject of the lavatorial. Birds had managed to imprison themselves within the glass edifice and were making a dreadful mess. Efforts were made to expel them but all failed. The queen sent for her old servant and, much embarrassed, haltingly tried to convey to the Duke the problem caused by bird droppings. 'Try sparrow hawks, ma'am' was his curt but essentially practical and successful advice.

History is not mathematics. It is all about more or less and rarely all or nothing. There were over the period outbreaks of civil stirrings occasionally political, for instance the Suffragette movement, but mainly to do with economic unrest and strike action. However, on the whole, by comparison with the previous century and a half, it was as if the tempest had been stilled and the waters were not rippled.

Policing had certainly improved. The Metropolitan Police was inaugurated in 1829; the Municipal Incorporation Act of 1835 introduced the borough forces and statutes in 1839 and 1856 established the county police services. By 1900 there were 38 county and 145 borough forces in England and Wales. The random mesh of gaols was nationalised in 1865 and replaced by a stable network of 95 prisons. This fabric of policing and prisons remained undisturbed until after the Second World War. Perhaps more important than the actual installation of police forces was the gradual consensus, apart from among the 'residuum' of the much reduced criminal fraternity, the police service negotiated with the public at large, The feared 'blue-butchers' slowly became friendly 'Bobbies'.

Crime declined rapidly, down, according to some commentators, by 50% in the latter half of the 19th century. Crime statistics are even more notoriously variable than cricket statistics but there is no doubt that by the last decades of the Victorian epoch crime had dropped to abnormally low not only by previous standards but by international yardsticks. In the last decades of the 19th century indictable offences had lessened to about 100,000 *per annum*, that is about two or three crimes for every thousand of the population – and that rate was to stay unchanged until the early 1960s. This was a very law-abiding community.

Sir William Harcourt, Home Secretary in William Gladstone's 1880/85 ministry, announced that the decrease in crime was 'a bright and encouraging sign on our social horizon'. In 1901 the *Criminal Register* noted that there was 'an approximation in the manners of different classes; a decline in the spirit of lawlessness.' Sir Richard Evans has recently drawn the significant conclusion that 'the more urban and industrialised an area became, the more its overall crime rate tended to fall'.[5]

The Victorian world was more settled and the old grey area between wrong- and right-doing had been clarified. Public space was more precisely regulated and life was led according to a more well-defined clock. The settled worker and his wife adopted more of the life-style of the middle-class gentleman and his family. Records from the 1880s show that 80% of marriages were of men and women who lived in the same district, a remarkable testimony to the stability of the labour market and the concomitant steadiness of housing tenure. The contrast with the restless, casual, inconstant character of work and accommodation of many people in the 18th century could not be more marked.

The respectability of the working-classes was thereby consolidated. The professional and managerial classes admired and encouraged this. They were more farsighted than their forefathers, sensing that a stolid plebeian phalanx was preferable to a belligerent one. Victor Gatrell in a 1996 article entitled *Crime, Authority and the Policeman State* wrote 'Victorians had no doubt that the best guarantee for the survival of their social order resided in the socialising of the poor rather than in their too candid disciplining.'[6] In this way the one class encouraged the other as the other sought to emulate the one. Both agreed on a temperate vision of a civil community based on mutual respect and recognition.

Among later professionals, church-going Jack Hobbs was one of a number who found little to complain of in the system, one in which, it is true, he had been immensely successful. It was a system that was a microcosm of the national pattern. He seems to have been one, for example, who very willingly accepted the role of the amateur, not least as captain. There are parallels in those other Victorian bastions of deeply etched tradition, the army and the stately home. In a county team and in some other cricketing situations where the gentry turned for technical succour from a paid expert, the relationship was akin to military rank or domestic service status. But, especially for the more senior pros, the grading was at non-commissioned officer level. The seasoned professional, like Wilfred Rhodes or George Hirst in the Yorkshire eleven, had much in common with the sergeant-major in the crack regiment or the butler in the big house, the Hudson of *Upstairs, Downstairs* or the Carson of *Downton Abbey*. The stairs might set apart servants from master and mistress, like the separate dressing rooms of the cricketers but both occupied the same edifice. Often the butlers and housekeepers or the sergeant majors and warrant officers held the honour of the house or regiment in higher esteem than their superiors, defending its conventions and peculiarities with a surprising fierceness. Thus was it with many cricket professionals, grimly protective of the ancient truths and habits of the game.

Even at a day-by-day practical level there was some humdrum rationale. Given the class division, the artisan in his soiled overall would not, even if suddenly gifted with a fortune, have felt comfortable entering a first-class railway carriage, sitting in the stands at a Football League ground or lounging in a stall seat at the Savoy Theatre. The lady of the house, had she been graciously trained in the courtesies, would have hesitated about bursting in on the servants' supper or at least would have apologised for so doing. The sergeants' mess was sacrosanct. No officer would have entered without the permit of the mess sergeant or regimental sergeant major. To stray into another profession, certainly until well after World War II, no right-thinking headmaster would have walked into the staff common room without a knock and polite request.

At the lowest stratum of practicality you couldn't easily let off steam about the boss or manager if he were alongside you. One may imagine the bastings many a naive young amateur skipper received unheard from his crusty professional colleagues shut away in their inferior but at least secluded dressing room. None of this proves the structure was morally pure. But it is worth seeing some of how it worked through contemporary eyes rather than through hindsight – and then there is a much more momentous issue.

That grand old recipe of good luck and good management kept Victorian Britain out of any serious military continental conflict that might have affected life at home. With, to do the Victorians justice, a little more of the latter management and a little less of the former luck, they preserved internal peace to an impressive degree and the reign of Queen Victoria enjoyed a domestic serenity lacking during the lives of her several Hanoverian predecessors. It is commonly accepted that this more stable background was a boon for the coming to fruition of spectator sports, chief among them at this juncture, cricket. Cause and effect in history rarely operates in a singular fashion. Usually there are reversals or spiral effects. Interaction is a well-used word in historical analysis. In a small but efficacious way the playing and watching of the style, mood and ethos of cricket that emerged in mid-19th century was part of the cause as well as an aspect of the effect. It contributed to the even and tolerant tenor that was so characteristic of the time.

In 1903 John Morley, Liberal statesman and Gladstone's biographer, delivered his trenchant verdict that since 1846 there had been 'not even a shadow of civic convulsion.' Cricket has not always had the pat on the bat it deserves for its decent role in the avoidance of civil convulsion.

1. Sandiford op.cit, pp. 112/127 for a meticulously researched and ingeniously argued account of this issue.
2. Keith Sandiford *English Cricket Crowds during the Victorian Age* in *Journal of Sports History* vol 9 no 3 1987.
3. Tony Laughton *Captain of the Crowd; Albert Craig, Cricket and Football Rhymester* (2008) pp. 195/198.
4. Peter Bailey (ed) *Music Hall; the Business of Pleasure* 1986.
5. Richard J.Evans *The Pursuit of Power; Europe 1815-1914* (2016) – and for valuable insights into the rise of the new elites, new industrial activities and new social manners across Europe, including the United Kingdom.
6. Victor Gatrell *The Hanging Tree; Execution and the English People 1770 to 1868* (2010) for an elaborate but lucid examination of this fundamental change.

Our picture gallery aims to illustrate the cross-class nature of
recreational cricket about half way through the period under review,
beginning with a smartly dressed gathering at Cranwell-on-Sea.
Included are a clergyman, as befits an age when church and
cricket were much entwined and, in the left background, a soldier,
another pertinent representative of cricket's following then.

A middle-class family outside their substantial dwelling in Kent.
Eleven 'gentlemen' are present, perhaps suggesting a cross-generational
kin team as was fielded by the Christopherson or Edrich families.
The ladies will be respectably supportive but, one
assumes, others will be making the tea.

THOLTHORPE . CRICKET TEAM 1924

The Tholthorpe club in North Yorkshire – seen in 1924 – with a doubtless well-earned cup; they were then playing in the Forest of Galtres League, Western Section. A tiny village of barely 300 residents, it is very likely the cricketers hailed from both class milieux. Their joint engagement in cricket masks the divide but there are sartorial hints; dark-coloured trousers and braces, for instance.

Similarly in this pleasant image of seventeen cricketing lads from Hooton Pagnell, near Doncaster; here the population was little more than 200 so again one may safely assume that practically all of the village boys are here a-cricketing. As with the Tholthorpe team, there is a social mixture, for which there are a few clues. The two wearing a watch and chain are unlikely to be working class whilst the wing collars may be another giveaway. Darker-coloured shirts and braces could be a working class pointer – but the important thing is that they are playing together.

Llwynpia C.C. – from the industrial valleys of Glamorgan – seen on their tour to Breconshire and Radnorshire over the Whitsun Bank Holiday of 1907. Although not veering too far from their roots, it allowed the workingmen to have a short break from their labours. Llywynpia demonstrates the rise and fall of cricket alongside the same industrial cycle. Its once rural population boomed after 1850 with the growth of coal mining and a cricket club was formed. One of it's leading figures, William Morgan played a leading role with Glamorgan CC, following the creation of the county club in July 1888, and he was instrumental in organising a trial match later that summer between the county and his club. In 1923 almost 3000 colliers were employed in the town; then the pits closed, the population fell, and the cricket club also folded. The county side though survived.

The Radcliffe club from Greater Manchester, seen above in 1911, was another example of industrial success besides, judging by the pavilion and seated spectators, civic pride, with a decent crowd assembled for an unpretentious local fixture. Like Llwynypia, Radcliffe had coal seams but it also prospered as a textile town, and this industrial mix meant it was luckier economically than Llwynypia. Although the cotton mills no longer whirr, its cricket club stands resplendent in the Central Lancashire League. Back in 1911, it played in the Bury Amateur League, employing one James Ingram as the professional. It was also a tennis club, a very middle-class game then.

*These cricketers in Dundee present a pretty picture.
Twelve angry young men, with not a pair of white flannels among them,
although most favour a regulation bow tie. The two youths swaddled in white
shrouds don't look old enough to be umpires in that day and age.
Remove the bats and pads and it could be a Wyatt Earp O.K.Corral vigilante
flash bulb photo for the Tombstone Gazette - yet it does illustrate the wide
spread of cricket then, regionally and generationally.*

*Finally, some cricket action, courtesy of the Earl Soham club during the 1930s.
An East Suffolk village of just a few hundred individuals, it is consequentially
probable that this is a cross-class team, their whites comfortably conveying that
sense of unison which is the essence of the 'class peace' theme of this text.*

Chapter Eight
Cricket and Class up to 1914

With little or no 'civil convulsion' and precious little military conflict abroad that troubled such domestic calm, industrialised Britain enjoyed, despite occasional setbacks, much economic prosperity. So it continued until the outbreak of the First World War. As for many decades the leading imperial as well as industrial power, the watchwords of the United Kingdom's economy were free trade, untramelled marketing and bold private entrepreneurship. This display of boundless activity, with its creed at one time summarised as 'Manchesterism' triumphant, is how Victorian Britain is recalled in the popular mind, and rightly so.

But there was another side to the national medallion, one duller and less exhilarating, that is perhaps less well remembered in the public consciousness. This was, from the 1830s onwards, the efforts of governments of all colours, to legislate for the encroachment of the state into the private realm and the erection of a fast growing public sector. At first sight, that marriage of a wholly free economy with a prominent public infrastructure may appear incompatible. Nevertheless, the Victorian authorities, their potency much boosted by reformed and energetic local government, were eager Collectivists. It was by no means altogether altruistic. The lesson had been learned, for example, that a decently housed work force, with fresh water and sanitation, was not only a healthier but a moderately more willing one, while the improvement of and the better cleansing of streets allowed quite literally for the wheels of commerce to run more freely.

From the viewpoint of the class divide, there was what the great social historian Asa Briggs called the 'many forces making for collaboration rather than confrontation', a movement which continued, as he succinctly traced, well into the 20th century.[1] This might be viewed as a virtuous spiral of government rewarding the working class for good conduct. The classic example is the gradual extension of the franchise. It is, for instance, generally accepted that the granting of the vote to urban workers in 1867 was influenced by the impressive peacefulness of the Lancashire mill-hands during the slump and famine consequent on the American Civil War and their resolve to uphold the moral case against slavery.

For their part governments seemed determined to ensure that, as modern facilities were introduced, working men and women would not be excluded. An act of 1844 insisted that every railway company should run what became known as a 'Parliamentary' train at least once a day on every route and service. The Libraries Act of 1850, which encouraged local authorities to levy a penny rate for the establishment of municipal libraries, was another instance, while William Gladstone's removal of what was called 'a tax on knowledge' is another. As Chancellor of the Exchequer he rid the nation of the advertisement tax, the newspaper stamp duty and the paper tax that a free press might flourish. It should be recalled that the installation of such taxes had been to halt the publishing of insurrectionary materials – rather like cricket clubs putting up the prices to deter the rougher sort - and thus their cancellation is an excellent illustration of the new trust in which the lower orders were being regarded.

There are illustrations galore but a very positive one was the introduction of the Penny Post in 1840. Before 1840 letters were charged according to distance and number of sheets. From here on in a penny would be the uniform cost for delivery anywhere in the country or, later, the Empire and the USA. The General Post Office delivered 132m letters in 1840, the first year of Rowland Hill's inventive scheme. In 1839 there had only been 75m letters delivered. By 1913 there were 300m letters posted. Prior to 1840 when the 'letter carrier' had being paid on delivery, costs were high, with, for example, 9d Birmingham to London among the standard charges. The equivalent of a reduction of the 1s3d it previously cost to send a letter to Glasgow from London to 1d would be if today the price of a first-class stamp fell from 64p to 4p. Moreover, far from taking the current market stance, the British government underwrote the new process until 1870 when it first began to realise a profit.

However, much as cricket teams and supporters benefited immeasurably from the railways, much as millions more were enabled to read avidly of their cricketing heroes' acts of glory in the cheap press and much as hard-pressed fixture and harassed team secretaries must have been eternally grateful for the advantages of the Penny Post, the most direct contribution of the nascent Collectivist state to cricket was the municipal park.

In 1834 a Select Committee of the House of Commons on drunkenness had strongly recommended the provision of 'public walks, or gardens, or open spaces for healthy and athletic exercise in the open air' and radical MPs like Joseph Hulme and Robert Slaney took up the cudgels. Soon forward-looking local authorities were taking as much pride in their parks as in their libraries, art galleries and museums. Park designers had what might appositely be called a field day. Among them were Joseph Paxton, creator of the Crystal Palace, John Gibson, Superintendent of London's parks, many of which had been in the royal gift, Edward Miller, who designed parks in Buxton, Halifax and Preston and Edward Vamp, responsible for Hesketh Park, Southport, Stanley Park, Liverpool and Birkenhead Park. Some parks were donated by or subscribed for by local philanthropy; Sir Robert Peel gave £10,000 towards the development of Peel Park, Salford.

The standard British park followed the landscaped enclave made popular earlier by Capability Brown and Humphrey Repton. Urban noises and bustle were effectively shut out of sight and mind by a surround of heavy foliage usually with ornate gates to feed the country estate fantasy. Inside this perimeter of bushes and trees was laid a Macadamised path known as a 'Brownean ring'. Within this circular walkway was the grassland. There was an occasional nod to the other two park typologies. The Italianate statement of a baroque focus for civil pride, like Florence's Boboli Gardens, was echoed in the bandstand that featured in most parks, while the Oriental attempt, as with the Taj Mahal, to create 'an oasis of beauty blooming in an earthly desert' was referenced in the colourful botanical gardens and flower beds that adorned many parks.

The park as a place to walk, listen to the band on a Sunday afternoon and look at the flowers was all very well. It suited the Victorian's pastoral dream that he was really a countryman at heart. It met the Victorian's wish to lure the working man away from the demon drink and the sin of idleness. An item in *the Times* in 1841 on the opening of the Regent's Park conveys this flavour admirably: 'the redemption of the working class through recreation' would now be possible as such people would benefit from 'the liberty of taking a walk in the more plebeian portions of the park, provided they had a decent coat on.'[2]

However, the evangelical concern with temperance and the chivalric yearning for pastoralism also underscored the school of thought that argued for rational recreation and public health. A sedate stroll was fine as far as it went – but it did not go very far in terms of active exercise; soon there were urgent pleas to deploy these often quite extensive green swards for games. There were obstacles. The most famed anti-cricket crusade was led by Lewis Carroll. In 1867 and 1879 he mounted attacks on Oxford University's desire to make the Parks the home of its cricket club. He parodied Oliver Goldsmith's *The Deserted Village* in his poem *The Deserted Parks*, claiming that the poor people of the town would lose out on their opportunities to enjoy a quiet promenade.

Interestingly, cricket was initially the main beneficiary, although football did catch up later with something of a vengeance. Cricket was the game with an Arcadian aura; football was still seen as rather a vulgar pastime. Cricket clubs in mid-19th century were more middle-class and better managed than what were often still somewhat unregulated football activities. One of the critical elements in the decisions to use parks for games was the rueful acknowledgment that it was preferable to license organised games rather than have mobs of youths causing havoc with disorganised ones.

There can be no doubt that there was a demand. In 1860 the newly opened Macclesfield Park played host to 40 or more cricket matches on Saturdays after the mills closed. In the year 1908 London County Council had 448 park pitches for 10,000 players and 30,000 fixtures. In some parks games were played serially, with some pre-breakfast starts to ensure all were accommodated. Some parks, of course – Stanley Park, Blackpool and Valentine's Park, Ilford are two of several - graduated to staging county cricket.

Jacques Carré, the French cultural historian and leading expert on the subject, wrote that as well as being 'a spectacular manifestation of Victorian civic art', parks were also 'a testing ground of the new urban ethos.' Parks proved to be a significant aspect of progressive local government and, in that they were made readily available for sport, they became the major contribution of municipal beneficence to the growth of cricket. This was the more especially so in that it allowed for the onset of less wealthy, by that token, more working-class orientated clubs. For example, many church-based clubs would have found it impossible to find the cost of a cricket ground at urban land values, plus the cash for the laying out and upkeep of the ground. The feasibility of renting a park pitch, ready mown and rolled, for a few hours' cricket opened the way for dozens more cricket clubs to flourish. Park cricket would continue to compose a marked segment of the recreational game for many years.

As the nation evolved into a more rational society with more bureaucratised practices, planned structures and well-defined mechanics in all parts of the community, the two salient and rapidly expanding classes appeared to find a similar definiteness in their own separate characterisation. It was more complex than the ancient lord of the manor and serf kind of relationship wherein master and servant were identified as high and low opposites. As the 19th century wore on, and although the superior/inferior mirroring did not vanish, these two classes adopted a much more knowing self-awareness. There was a growing consciousness of what it intrinsically meant to be a class member irrespective of relativity to other classes.

Anthony Trollope delineated the Victorian 'gentleman' with masterful craft and precision. 'The one great line of demarcation in the world', he wrote, 'was that which separated gentlemen from non-gentlemen.' There were codes that were instinctively de-cyphered. They touched on dress, gesture, patterns of speech, social and other tastes and a whole series of reference points by which one gentleman recognised another. In Trollope's *The Last Chronicle of Barset* (1867) the impoverished Josiah Crawley, Vicar of St Ewold's is embarrassed by his lack of money when discussing the marriage of his daughter to the son of the wealthy Archdeacon Theophilus Grantly. The Archdeacon sought to put him at his ease. "We stand', said he, 'on the one level ground on which such men can meet each other. We are both gentlemen."

As the 20th century dawned, about 9.5m fell into the category of gentlemen and their families living in their, increasingly, suburban homes. Some earned no more than £150 *per annum* but the majority had yearly salaries of between £300 and £500 and were able to afford the £30 or £40 rentals for a small house in the environs of London. Having domestic servants was one much sought after criterion of gentlemanliness and ladylikeness. According to the wise Mrs Isabella Beeton's *Household Management*, first published in 1861 but with lots of editions long after her early death, those on an income of £1000 might hope to hire five servants and those on £200 one servant and maybe a part-timer. Even Josiah Crawley had one servant as did the insolvent Mr Micawber, namely, 'a' Orfling' from St Luke's Workhouse. Some 300,000 of these gentlemanly breadwinners were in the church, medical, legal and administrative professions, 150,000 in banking and 200,000 in education but with a huge number, no less than

1.5m, in the clerical and retail trades. A particular growth area was among the professional as opposed to the commercial ranks.

There remained immense social pressure on the middle-class family, whatever its income, to sustain the pretension of that status. The American comic strip in the *New York* Globe, later a cartoon film, 'Keep up with the Jones' made its opportune entry in 1913. Turning again to fiction for pictorial support, Leonard Bast, the hapless young clerk with confused dreams of artistic enhancement in E.M Forster's 1910 novel *Howard's End,* 'lived at the extreme verge of gentility' and he was by no means alone. A more cheerful illustration comes from H.G.Wells. From his own painful experience and using his own feckless father, Joseph (four wickets in four balls for Kent v Sussex in 1862 in one of his eight first-class matches) as the model, he published, also in 1910, *The History of Mr Polly*. Please note it is the history of Mr not Alfred Polly, acknowledging that convivial individual's desperate aspiration to a genteel ranking.

In this same Edwardian period the working class numbers had also grown, if not quite so swiftly, to 28.5m inclusive of families. Overall, and in spite of the usual ups and downs of the economy, wages had been augmented and there had even been a slight decline in prices and rents. By 1910 the wage range was from 18s a week for unskilled workers to a much more healthy £2.5s for skilled tradesmen. Expert opinion suggested that 30s for a 48 hours working week was a reasonable minimum income for an average family. The major groupings of workers were, predictably, 5m in manufacturing, over half of these in textiles; a rising figure of 2m in domestic service; a receding figure of not much more than 1m in agriculture; 0.5m miners and about the same in transport and the building trades, and roughly 1m in miscellaneous trades.[3]

Those few figures give some idea of how the new working class fell into certain mainstream sectors and, as the heat of early industrialisation cooled and there was a general settlement of social and economic existence, these workers grew ever more willing to subscribe to the craft unions that represented them and the friendly societies that brought them succour in hard times. There was a devout wish to present a peaceable countenance. It is a terrible gloss on the Peterloo Massacre that many, including young women, had decked themselves in their best finery, regarding the occasion as a day out, not a violent insurrection. Furthermore, following the tumult of Peterloo, the radical leader Samuel Bamford caught up with the fleeing contingents in the Harpurhey outskirts of Manchester, reformed a thousand of them into file and marched them home 'to the sound of fife and drum, with our only banner waving.' Discipline and good order held steady on the one side, and, on the other, as E.P Thompson points out, future governments would think twice about a martial response and 'never since Peterloo has authority dared to use equal force against a peaceful English crowd.' Ironically, in the past such gatherings had been scorned for their wildness; when they marched in smart procession, insensitive magistrates had been even more frightened.

There was still much mutual comprehension to be negotiated. Activism on the one side and over-robust reaction on the other never vanished completely but the temper of the age mellowed remarkably. Slowly the trades unions won reputable status and legal recognition. By 1914 the number of trades unionists affiliated to the Trades Union Congress was over 4m, a half the labour force and overwhelmingly skilled craftsmen. The friendly societies such as the Oddfellows, the Buffaloes and the Foresters had getting on for 6m members and total funds of £41m. Along with the network of co-operative societies, these activities provided hundreds of men and women with experience of handling accounts and running institutions. When it came to organising a cricket club, many working class men were more used to formal procedure than many of their middle-class colleagues.

What is of moment in the growing sense of class strength among the labour force is the pride in which it was held, no more so than in the ranks of the cricketing professionals, proud of their hard-honed skills and quietly self-satisfied in the esteem with which they were held in their local communities. In the winter months the ex-miners and ex-spinners, that is of the textile genre, would stroll through the cobbled streets of their home environs, knowing that they were admired, if not fussily, by their neighbours. They had, as the saying went, 'got on.'

No less than with the new middle-classes, the self-awareness of the industrial working class derived from men who believed they had deliberately attained class consciousness. Unlike the serf or the peasant of previous historical epochs, a class tag had not been thrust upon them by their superiors as a derogatory label. Here were working people determined to shake off the image of their being an uncouth rabble, as Samuel Bamford had endeavoured to do on St Peter's Fields, Manchester in 1819. His instruction had read 'It was deemed expedient that the meeting should be as morally effective as possible...We had frequently been taunted in the press with our ragged dirty appearance...with the confusion of our proceedings and the mob-like crowds in which our members were mustered.'

Sobriety and cleanliness would be the watchwords, with self-education the means and self-respect the characteristic to be admired. Coupled with that growing class discipline was a less clamorous and insurgent appeal. The more sensible constitutional and social reforms sought no longer had the ring of French Revolutionary fervour and audacity. 'This collective self-consciousness', concluded E.P.Thompson, 'was indeed the great spiritual gain of the Industrial Revolution...forming their own traditions of mutuality in the friendly societies and trades clubs, these men did not pass, in one generation, from the peasantry to the new industrial town. They suffered the experience of the Industrial Revolution as free-born Englishmen.'[4]

As the franchise was widened, the political parties, no more chiefly loose groupings often of friends and families, felt under pressure to develop more formal mechanisms. Although the Liberal Party was strongly supported by working men loyal to Gladstone, 'the People's William', the astute Disraeli was busily acquiring a working-class vote for the Conservative Party that it never wholly lost. His *Times* obituary in 1881 included the famous phrase that he 'saw the Conservative in the working-class voter as the sculptor saw the angel in the marble.' It was in his honour and named after his favourite flower that the Primrose League was launched in 1883 as a mass movement backing Toryism which peaked at 2m members in the Edwardian era. The Primrose League was suffused in medievalist imagery. It had 'habitations' such as the 'King Athelstan' Habitation at Malmesbury or the 'Coningsby' equivalent at Brighton and 'tributes', a humble threepence annually, where lesser mortals had to suffice with branches and subscriptions.

This well-marshalled army of volunteers did much political canvassing and also enjoyed a range of social activity. It was open to everyone apart from 'atheists and enemies of the British Empire' and is a picturesque example of the merging of the classes, for not the least of its attractions was the chance for lower middle and upper working class men and women to decorously rub occasional shoulders with the titled and belted lords and ladies. Its *faux*-medievalism is a further reminder of the chivalric nature of Victorian national character.

Having been enfranchised by the 1867 Reform Act, my great-grandfather, a chief ostler with the Bridgewater and then the Manchester Ship Canal Companies was numbered among this noble company but perhaps more relevant to immediate matters is that Lord Harris was a rather more well-known member. He was Chancellor of the Primrose League in 1887, 1888 and 1896 and its 1894 *Manual* defined his values precisely: 'bringing high and low, rich and poor together, breaking down social barriers and uniting all classes in a common crusade against the forces of atheism and revolution'.

For all its air of patronage and, perhaps worse, its avoidance of fundamental social reforms, Lord Harris overtly saw a parallel in his fair dealings with respectable cricket professionalism, regarding cricket as 'a great Conservative institution', without apology for the capital 'C'. Lord Hawke, his colleague in their little campaign to have paid cricketers treated more kindly in so far as they made manifest a seemly reputability, wrote in his memoirs in exactly the same vein, even wordage: 'high and low, rich and poor, greet one another practically on an equality, and sad will be the day for England if socialism ever puts class v class and thus ending sports which have made England.'[5]

If the Conservatives contributed the chivalry, the Liberals were heavier on the evangelical front, reliant as they were on a formidable nonconformist adherence. Several professional cricketers were of this persuasion. A well-turned anecdote of a slightly later vintage epitomises that condition. The stout Lancashire spin bowler and safe slip catcher, Richard Tyldesley, called back a batsman in a county game after he had been given out caught by him. Both umpire and batsman were content with the decision but Dick Tyldesley believed he had feathered the ground with the ball. At close of play Neville Cardus asked him why, given the general opinion favoured a just catch, he had so acted.

'Westhoughton Sunday School, Mr Cardus', muttered Tyldesley, 'Westhoughton Sunday School.' This may well have been a sample of Mr – all the pros apparently called him Mr in every statement – Cardus's' artistic truth. It may well have been the writer's version of what Richard Tyldesley tried to express or perhaps no more than an assumption on his part of what had passed through the catcher's mind and conscience. What cannot be doubted is the truth of the meaning of the story and the stern ethical code inbred by the chapels of the industrial townships.

By way of reinforcement from pre-1914 days, J.T.Tyldesley was a dedicated Independent Methodist. Lancashire were blessed with two branches of the Tyldesley clan, John Thomas being of the Worsley variant. Apart from his religious beliefs, he is of interest as being the one professional batsman of his generation to stand comparison with the majestic amateurs of his time. In the first two Tests of the 1902 series against Australia he was the only paid batsman in the top five, appearing in the order after Archie MacLaren, C.B.Fry K.S.Ranjitsinhji and Hon. F.S.Jackson. He was described as a 'Player' who batted like a 'Gentleman', a considerable compliment and a tribute to amid, a clutch of skills, his dextrous quick-footedness. This agility he ascribed to whirling around dance floors with those he reported as having been 'buxom Lancashire lassies.' Possibly it was the Independent Methodism that gave him the quiet composure for which he was also renowned.

What might, with a massaging of the imagination, be called the chivalric amateurs and the evangelical professionals came together in unison at the Oval in 1912 in what proved to be the last home Test before the onset of World War I. The first 'timeless' Test, it drew to conclusion the rather lacklustre triangular tournament of that summer with Australia and South Africa involved. England beat Australia by 244 runs.

The England team was comprised of four gentlemen and seven players, almost a perfect replica of the national class demographic. The amateurs were C.B.Fry, R.H.Spooner, J.W.H.T.Douglas and F.R.Foster, a quartet of sportmen of splendid ability who might have been hand-picked to personify the Corinthian spirit of cricket's Golden Age. The professionals were Jack Hobbs, Wilfred Rhodes, Frank Woolley, Middlesex's J.W. Hearne, E.J. 'Tiger' Smith, the Warwickshire wicket keeper, Harry Dean, the Lancashire quick bowler, and that most indefatigably independent of professionals, Sydney Barnes. Again they might have been chosen to represent both the rare talent and the serious application of the paid cricketing brethren. Several of the eleven remain household names among today's cricket buffs; then, all of them would have been liberally heralded in the sporting pages of the press.

Stretch the imagination further and and envision them preparing for the game, four in the stronghold of one dressing room, seven in the fortress of another. Possibly the amateurs discussed affairs of the day. On the first day of the match the Frenchman Adolphe Pegoud performed the first parachute jump in Europe and that may have tickled their sportive nerve. Possibly the professionals discussed cricketing matters. The manner in which the Australians were treated as amateurs but somehow ended up earning money was always a sore point. Wilfred Rhodes for one ever felt the ambiguity of being famous and yet somehow servile, because of being on low pay but it never altered his earnest commitment to his trade. Then they all emerged either individually to bat or as two groups to field. England won the toss and the eleven batted, shared partnerships and then fielded and bowled as a team without rancour or demur.

This more peaceable ambiance reigned at the Oval and across the land. Whilst the lines of social separation remained clear and imperishable, and although, not least in those immediate pre-war years, there were occasional sparks of political and economic fury, in daily practice both these main social groupings tended to adopt the same set of values in regard of family and community life, religious and moral observance, political affiliation and belief, leisure pursuits and general disposition. There was class peace rather than class war,

In 1915 Harold Brighouses's deliciously crafted play *Hobson's Choice*, set in 1880, was first performed. The Lear-like figure of Henry Hobson the complacent Salford shoe shop owner, soon to be outwitted by Maggie, his eldest of three daughters, grandly declaimed his beliefs near the opening of the play: 'I'm Hobson, I'm middle-class and proud of it. I stand for common sense and sincerity...You forget the majesty of trade and the unparalleled virtues of the British constitution which are all based on the sanity of the middle-class, combined with the diligence of the working classes.'

The cross-classed audiences in the stalls and galleries of several repertory theatres that over the years laughed at the opinionated bumptiousness of Mr Hobson nonetheless agreed with the sentiment he expressed.

1. Asa Briggs *A Social History of England* (1983).
2. Jacques Carré *People's Parks; the Design and Development of Victorian Parks in Britain* 'Journal of Garden History' (April 2012).
3. Donald Read *England 1868-1914; the Age of Urban Democracy* (1979) for much of this previous discussion. This is an erudite and wide-ranging book – with a perceptive sub-title.
4. E.P.Thompson *The Making of the English Working Class* (1963) for an absorbingly epic account of this process.
5. Sissons op.cit. pp. 89-90 in particular.

Chapter Nine
Cricket and Class in the Inter-War Years

The 1914-18 War plays a significant role in the history of English cricket but it is a very negative one. This terrible conflict was the subject of two pieces of inaction on the part of the cricketing authorities. Both stemmed from the view of cricket as not so much a sport as the physical expression of moral worth. The first was the decision to halt first-class cricket for the duration and the second was the determination not to taint cricket by the slightest modification thereafter.

One senses the impression that the decision to forego first-class cricket for the duration was not taken because cricket was trivial; far from it. It was so important that it was impossible to contemplate fighting a war and celebrating an ethical imperative at one and the same time. First-class cricketers were keen to volunteer and, indeed, were placed under intense social and economic pressure so to do. MCC ditched its extraordinary lengthy list of 163 fixtures and just played about 30 matches against public schools, fielding teams entirely composed of medically unfit members or those too ancient to be called to the colours. The northern leagues survived to some extent, justified in terms of providing relief for weary war workers, and some county players combined such war work with such weekend cricket.

Most poignant at all, those hundreds of public schoolboys who had been instructed on the greensward on long afternoons by grumpy old cricket professionals had also been drilled on the quadrangles and in the gymnasia for similar periods by grizzled old army NCOs. Such cadetship meant almost instant commissioning as a second lieutenant and a lodgement as platoon commander in the trenches. Scores of *Wisden* obituaries over those grim years testify to the deaths of young amateurs, some with no more than their schools colours as their cricketing accreditation. There were 400 such notices taking up 60 pages in the 1917 annual while Peter Wynne-Thomas has calculated that one in eleven contemporary first-class cricketers was slain.[1]

The holy writ of cricket, the outward and visible sign of the inward grace of Christianity mediated by Englishry, loomed large amid the register of values for which the war was fought. For all the empty, vain talk of change and 'homes fit for heroes to live in', the dominant tenor of the establishment was the restoration of the *status quo ante bellum*. Fazed and shocked by the butchery of the carnage, this desire to return to the past, to what, however mistakenly, was imagined to be the sylvan Edwardian summers of yesteryear, was palpable. There was scarcely a blasphemous whisper of reform. No one sought to seize the opportunity to take a long look and to re-build. Cricket was sports' Peter Pan, a play and novel written by J.M.Barrie, himself a cricket enthusiast, in the decade before the war. The cricket authorities looked back to their own Neverland of a self-ascribed Golden Age and believed that the game had achieved perfection and need not mature any more. Thus cricket, like Peter Pan, never grew up. It was locked in a prism of the past.

The ever percipient Gerald Howat called the inter-wars years the Second Golden Age. It was in format and style almost exactly the same as the first one, with the added good fortune that, happily, there were players of dazzling brilliance to adorn it.[2] After the many changes of the more bustling and self-confident Victorian age, cricket was deemed godlike in perfection; to meddle with it was heresy. For example, after some jockeying of counties over the years, the sixteen championship counties of 1914 were duly concretised as if in stone. Over the next hundred and more years there would be but the two additions of Glamorgan in 1921 and Durham in 1992 and, even more significantly, no subtractions.

It followed inexorably that there would be no change in the Gentleman/Player distinction nor yet in the steadfast alliance of the amateur and professional in the first-class game. Over the seasons there was a slight decline in the number of amateurs but the counties clung desperately to the convention of, at the very least, an amateur captain. Moreover, the unchanged cloisters of the public schools and Oxbridge continued untouched and the stream of handsome young Varsity batsmen was sustained for another half century. That said, the insistence on the officer-class captain meant that counties sometimes resorted to selecting an amateur not really worthy of a place in the team, itself a parody of the Great War trope of an experienced NCO in contempt of a fresh-faced, ingenuous officer. That fine example of Yorkshire and England doughtiness Maurice Leyland caustically said of his county's championship triumphs in the 1920s and 1930s that they won them all with ten men.

The vocational background of professional cricketers has been analysed a little and the predominance of entries from the upper or skilled ranks of the working classes observed. Thus far the amateur cohort has been treated amorphously as if the middle-class were one shapeless mass. At this juncture it might be timely to examine the vocational gradings of the amateur players.

From a broad, sweeping scrutiny but by no means an ironclad piece of scientific research, of 1000 or so *Wisden* obituaries of amateur cricketers it has been possible to draw a sketch of their careers and how they earned their money. Not all were first-class cricketers but they had all done sufficiently well in the game to be selected for the *Wisden* accolade. Moreover, the total does not include the First World War deaths which would have very much distorted the picture in terms of military engagement.[3]

A good many had no specific vocational reference, indicating that, as one would expect, quite a few amateurs did live off unearned income or vague family business funding. Some professions do not show conspicuously, among them the arts, politics, medicine and law. There are notable exceptions. Sir Charles Aubrey Smith of Cambridge University, England and Hollywood remains the most well-known actor-cricketer, while William Yardley, Cambridge University, Kent and the Gentlemen, was a colourful writer of burlesques and farces. Francis Worsley, rather better recalled as the producer of the iconic wartime radio comedy show *ITMA*, played a couple of times for Glamorgan.

Lord Harris and Sir Stanley Jackson are probably the two who managed to combine cricketing glory with high-ranking political appointments but, given the association of cricket with imperialism, there are relatively few politically-orientated cricketers. Perhaps it was asking too much of colonial officers to excel in the domestic game. There have been cricketing M.Ps, such as the Cambridge blue Sir Hubert Ashton, one of a famous cricket family, and Peter Eckersley, who captained Lancashire, while Hon. George Lyttelton, another Cambridge blue and from another well-known cricketing clan, was chief private secretary to William Gladstone. Given the prominence of the Grace family and medicine, it is surprising to find doctors and surgeons in short supply on the first-class cricket field. Lawyers, too, are not heavily represented; A.G.Steel Q.C of Lancashire and England is possibly the most notable 'legal' cricketer; he illustrates the reason for the dearth of his ilk - he found it well- nigh impossible to juggle cricket and the law.

Predictably enough, the army, the church and the teaching profession dominate the list. Two-fifths of the number reviewed were military men and a quarter either churchmen or teachers or in some cases both. Foremost in the long procession of soldiers on cricketing duties would be the then so-called 'soldier-batsmen' such as W.L.Foster, one of the Worcestershire brotherhood, and R.H.Spooner of Lancashire and England. In 1899 at Taunton against Somerset R.H.Poore, who became a Brigadier-General and Captain E.G.Wynyard put together a record sixth wicket stand of 411 for Hampshire. That was a glittering display of the army's contribution to cricket.

David Sheppard, Bishop of Liverpool, was but the last in a remarkable lineage of clergyman-cricketers. A resounding example of the combined role might be Rev. Vernon Royle, the Oxford University and Lancashire player and resplendent cover point, who became headmaster of Stanmore Park School. The Rev. Edward Lyttelton, a further representative of that well-known family, taught at Wellington and Eton and then was headmaster of Haileybury before returning to Eton as headmaster. He played for Cambridge University and Middlesex.

It is apparent that these three professions of army, clergy and teaching were the most feasible callings in terms of finding time to play cricket. Hampshire benefited from the proximity of Aldershot when it came to selecting 'soldier batsmen', officers who might be granted leave for cricketing purposes; school-teachers had a long summer holiday and it was not unknown for schools to give a talented teacher leave for the summer term; whilst the cynically inclined might suggest that vicars and curates only worked on Sundays when first-class cricket was forbidden.

Needless to say, there was some grumbling among the professionals when such amateurs turned up and the pros found they were dropped at the cost of their match fee. There were also some complaints that amateurs always managed to be available for the seaside resort fixtures and were somehow otherwise engaged when it was time for the tough northern tour. Despite such doubtings, the evidence does appear to confirm fairly conclusively that many amateurs who made a contribution to the process and styling of English cricket had a military, clerical and educational background. In practical terms this suggests the obvious comment that those with such vocational duties found it simpler to fit in some first-class cricket but it does resonate with the earlier claim made in chapter four that those responsible for the spread of cricket in mid-Victorian times were of a similar background.

But there lay a riddle at the heart of English cricket that remains unsolved unto this very day. For all its success in and contribution to English society in the Victorian era, a question mark already hung over the sport. As if in some Greek or Shakespearean tragedy, the hallmark of its strength was also the harbinger of its weakness. Perhaps Hamlet's hesitant uncertainty comes closest to a theatrical analogy of cricket's ambivalent position.

Without the potent force of middle-class and upper-class involvement it is doubtful whether cricket would have survived as a nationally ubiquitous activity with a spectator base, widespread engagement in every part of the country and a supportive press and literary backing. A colourful rider to the situation was the fashion in which foreign visitors were surprised, even shocked, in pre-1914 days by the sight of working men paying their sixpences to be entertained by an Indian prince who was prepared to place himself on exotic show. But the construct was always from one important standpoint decidedly rickety. Cricket, as it had evolved, was not commercially viable and therein lay the seeds of its own likely decline, even collapse.

There were practical as well as ethical issues. Lost in the wonder of it all, the cricketing powers-that-be had somehow neglected to observe the extension of the passage of time it took to complete a cricket match. In the formative Hanoverian years a day, granted fine weather, was usually adequate for four innings to be negotiated with totals of 30 or 40 commonplace. The improvement of grounds and the predominance of batting slowly led to much higher scores. An oddity of first-class cricket is that the gamut of innings totals is extreme, running from 12 to 1107. No other game at its premier levels offers such variance. Because commercial income did not have the prior call, little was done – and five day, even timeless, Tests were one consequence.

Most sports either have a given target – the first to reach 501 in darts or the best over eighteen holes of golf - or a specified time limit – as in football or hockey. Cricket was much more open than that and no one had the temerity to intervene. Gradually during the 19th century, as a result of so many 'unfinished' games, the practice grew, much affirmed by the league format, of playing just half a match, that is, one innings each. The splendid concept of the second chance was thereby removed and a system evolved whereby first-class cricket had a totally different formula from most of the recreational game, rather as if professional football might last 90 minutes and amateur football only 45 minutes.

The practice of players getting themselves out deliberately in order to attempt to bowl out the other side in a three day match led to the declaration law of 1889. It was only permissible to invoke this regulation on the third day but it does demonstrate how the glut of runs was continuing to play havoc with the allotted time. This tension between the completion of a match and the time duration available made for a rather unattractive commercial proposition.

Turning to the all-encompassing nature of every English first-class team in the senior echelon being based on a membership club linked with a county, this created a most inward-looking pattern. The subscribing gentlemen quite correctly and legitimately ran these clubs for their own benefit, often acquiring professional help of working class vintage in so doing. As the members, through subscriptions and frequently by bailing out contributions, kept these cricketing ships afloat, they were entirely within their rights to withstand attempts to alter the clubs' profile, say, with profits in mind.

It is palpably obvious that, as of 1919, seventeen clubs, not all of them sensibly located from a business viewpoint, all controlled at the behest of and on behalf of a relatively small cohort of upper and middle class gentlemen, and playing a lengthy series of eighteen-hour fixtures, was a cockeyed scheme from a purely commercial standpoint. This, equally obviously, had ramifications, for the work-force of professionals who helped to shore up this tottering edifice.

It tottered but never collapsed, for the eagerness of its dedicated upper crust adherents was usually, with the aid of their resources and resourcefulness, adequate to avoid extinction. The chivalric-cum-evangelical fervour prevailed. Yet it was this very ethos that wavered when faced with the harsh countenance of hard coin. The pastoral fallacy won through again, hinting at the ugliness of the commercial world while enjoying its advantages, almost akin to the Victorian approach to the new-fangled water closet – happy to use it as long as no one mentioned it.

Cricket was not the only manifestation of this sentiment. Perhaps buoyed by the return of the United Kingdom to the free market neo-liberalism that had marked the Hanoverian period, there was a serious academic debate in the last quarter of the 20th century on this very topic. It was vigorously argued, if not without challenge, that there had been a disdain of industry, technology and money-making that had led to economic decline or, at least, a failure to realise the maximum possibilities of such enterprise. It was claimed that the establishment and, crucially, its public school values, was responsible for the belief that dirtying one's hands commercially was hardly suitable employment for a gentlemen.[4]

Certainly there was between the wars a determined resolve to keep cricket clean of the damaging effects of the profit motive that it might retain its moral sheen. In press commentaries on suggestions or wishes to lighten up or popularise the game it is interesting to remark on the use of 'circus' as the likely outcome of such debasement. Of much relevance to this study, there is an equally consistent theme of the value of the amateur in guaranteeing the degree of purity so admired by cricket lovers. Amateurs were the standard bearers of the moral virtue of the game. More mundanely, even allowing for some being in receipt of often exorbitant expenses, fielding many amateurs did help to lower the wage bill.

It would be difficult to visualise a more non-commercial condition. The system was not a feasible money-making proposition and the cricketing oligarchs who ran the system were anti-trade. The weather factor was another perverse risk; the heat of 1921 brought 285,000 paying customers to Yorkshire's home fixtures; a moist 1922 saw that total fall to not many more than 200,000. As today, Test receipts helped but these, too, were variable; Bradman's 1934 Australians were the reason why £45,000 was doled out to the counties in 1934, following a rather more fallow 1933 when there was not much more than £5000 available after the then not over-strong West Indians had been the tourists.

In effect, the counties struggled through the inter-wars years to maintain financial viability.[5] Essex had losses in twelve, Kent in seven, Lancashire in six and the highly successful Yorkshire in three seasons. In 1936 only three counties made a surplus. There continued to be a reliance on what in the theatre would be termed 'angels'. Such haloed figures included Sir Julien Cahn who gave generously to both Nottinghamshire and Leicestershire; the businessman Alfred Cockerill who donated an estimated £10,000 to Northants, and the Fry chocolate company who purchased the Gloucestershire county ground at Bristol and let it out free to the club. Bazaars and concerts, the sort of social fund-raising events which would more normally be associated with a local church, were organised at the summer's end to fend off the wolf from the pavilion door. Today's sponsorship may be more focused and graphic; it is not unprecedented.

There was any amount of tinkering in the 1920s and 1930s, perhaps illustrating the tremulous, nervy yet peculiarly timid mood of Britain in that period which one of its best historians David Thomson called 'incorrigible *immobilism'*. The minimum number of matches played varied and counties had shorter and longer fixture lists while eight different scoring devices were used to make some sense of so flexible a competition. There was some slight meddling with the laws but, apart from the application of the LBW ruling to balls pitched on the off side, there was nothing much that endured. Birth or residence continued to control the destiny of the professional, although the amateur enjoyed some leeway by way of eligibility.

In 1937 MCC and the County Advisory Committee set up the Findlay Commission to examine these matters but the outcome was less than revolutionary. Any thought of two day or divisional cricket was dismissed out of hand and Sunday cricket was not even raised as a fit subject for discussion. One of the wry curiosities of the age was the cricket authorities' constant complaint about having to pay Entertainment Tax. Their plea was a virtual admission that cricket did not fall under that heading.

Picking an average mid-wars season by way of exemplification, there were 296 first-class matches played in the British Isles in 1936, half as many again as were played in 1900. A rough estimate would suggest that 1.4m attended these matches, comprised of 1.2m paying customer at all the county games, another 200,000 spectators either at other first-class fixtures or, with a wild guess, that phantom figure of subscribing members. The total number of county members at this time was around 50,000, ranging from 2000 or so at Derbyshire or Essex to 6500 at Yorkshire but evidence as to their actual pavilion appearances is almost non-existent.

Although many more games were played and the national population was bigger in 1936 than 1900 when 1.5m, as described in chapter seven, watched first-class cricket, it appears that cricket gates fell slightly in these years, perhaps the more so in the 1930s than the 1920s. Indeed, one of the drivers of the Findlay Commission was, of course, the perceived fall in attendances that led to financial woes. This might partially be explained by the dire economic conditions of the depression years, although the effects were patchy in incidence as to region and type of industry. For instance some light industrial businesses did well while the 1930s slump damaged what was a low wage, low price economy; the differential between working and being on the dole in monetary terms was much narrower than, say, in any of the major post-1945 recessions.

It must be emphasised that the almost unconscious and certainly unplanned upper tier of cricket, not least with its unusual compromises of class distinction at player and spectator level, had never been less than precarious. It had never been self-financing and had always been in need of patronage or other additional fund raising. In the inter-wars decades it was the same, possibly a little worse, and with little hint of any development.

Conversely, league cricket prospered. Jack Williams has astutely demonstrated the strength of league support at this time, arguing that overall it rivalled and often surpassed county spectatorship. The fourteen clubs of the Lancashire League attracted as many as 350,000 and never less than 172,000 paying adherents in these years; the Central Lancashire League gates have been estimated at 330,000 over a season, an average of 2000 a match; the Bradford League returned figures of well over 200,000, and the Yorkshire Council League numbers have been estimated to be double that. Large and active memberships then added to these figures.[6]

The presence of Learie Constantine as Nelson's professional is the prime example of how the league clubs sought to thrive. In 1934 when Nelson played their arch-rivals Colne in the Worsley Cup Final there were 14,000 present and well-supported league clubs drew up to as many as 75,000 customers in a good year. It cannot be doubted that the huge majority of these were working class in origin and that they viewed their Saturday afternoon sixpenny cricketing venture much as they saw their winter outing to watch Blackburn Rovers or Bolton Wanderers. The one way in which cricket contrived to stay ahead of football – and it did so without conscious public relations effort – was to preserve the myth that football should not be played in summer. It was over a hundred years before the penny dropped and football encroached on the cricket season without fear of players collapsing with dehydration in the ferocious heat of the English summer.

There is evidence that some non-league clubs enjoyed decent crowds, sometimes a few hundreds even at a village match and reaching some thousands for high-quality suburban and metropolitan teams. It is likely that these crowds were socially mixed, perhaps with an accent on middle class representation. At county level there is evidence that 10% to 15% of the gate income was for the stands, suggesting that these would have been middle class patrons. One must add to this the members in the pavilions, the trickiest of calculations given the lack of such records. However, a reasonable guess is that together the members and the higher payers approached the 20% or 25% of the crowd that allows one to point to the microcosm of a 25/75 class split remaining consistent.

Recreational cricket remained in good health between the two wars. Allowing a wide margin either side, it might be intrepidly stated that some 250,000 adults were engaged in playing cricket each weekend of the season. It is difficult to guess at the number of actual teams. One helpful guide is the fact that just prior to World War II there were well over a thousand clubs in the home counties affiliated to Club Cricket Conference, most of which fielded at least two elevens, suggesting a gross sum of perhaps 2500 teams. Many clubs provided the basic equipment and kept the subscriptions low, so that there was a decent welcome for working class enthusiasts. Playing conditions were frequently primitive and costume was not always *à la mode,* but thousands contrived to be involved in the game.

There is some evidence that, predictably, blue collar workers outnumbered unskilled labourers, a feature noted in Victorian times. It should be recalled that few of these adults would have played cricket at school, unlike their middle class team-mates or opponents. Schools cricket did expand between the wars – for example by 1937 there was the amazing total of 180 schools playing in the Liverpool schools competition – but throughout the country the incidence of elementary school cricket was decidedly hit and miss. The major problem in urban districts was the lack of school playing fields.

Unlike the narrow format of county cricket, recreational sides sprang from any number of sources, with works team, understandably, often a little more handsomely endowed than others. Having earlier described the religious aura in which Victorian cricket was suffused, it is proper to underline the continuing influence of the churches. Cricket flourished yet still as a pastoral expression of a religion that was believed in or accepted by all classes; it was Christianity at the crease. In Bolton, Burnley and Oldham in the early 1920s 258 out of the 395 teams – itself an impressive total - were church based. This was singular but not wholly so; many areas had a goodly proportion of church clubs and some districts were able to arrange local leagues solely for Sunday Schools, just as there were specialist works leagues, the collieries around Mansfield being a sturdy example of a competition involving pits only.

If there were some evangelical substance in that ecclesiastical continuum, there was likewise no diminution in the chivalric rural dream, with village green cricket celebrated in the flesh and in the word, the bat and the pen equally embroiled. Sometimes the two were in concert. J.C.Squire, poet and critic and the Mr Hodge of A.G.Macdonell's much-loved *England, their England* team is a case in point. Leader of the Invalids touring *literati* eleven, he lovingly adhered to the 'rural root' of the game, for, he argued, 'few men...would not rather play on a field surrounded by ancient elms and rabbit-haunted bracken than on a better field with flat black lands or gasworks around.' W.G.Grace and Don Bradman might be numbered among those few men but it was an honest enough sentiment for the recreational cricketer.

Literature between the wars provides several illustrations of rural cricket, many of them with class undertones and occasionally overtones. A couple of examples are E.M.Forster's *Maurice* written and located in 1913/14, revised in 1932 and 1959/60 but not published, because of its homosexual content until 1971 after his death, and L.P.Hartley's *The Go-between*, published in 1953 but set in the days of the Boer War. Both have episodes based, not on country house matches as such, but on 'hall' and village annual matches, meaning that the stately home eleven includes servants. Thus the eponymous Maurice, a gentleman visitor and reluctant member of the 'Park' eleven, has a profitable partnership with the footman Alec with whom on the preceding evening he had formed a passionate gay relationship. The night's shared excitement prefigures the day's cricket in alliance. It is reminiscent of all those Talbot Baines Reed *The Fifth Form at St Dominic's* typology of school stories which end in a cricket match in which two close friends – Oliver Greenfield and Horace Wraysford in the St Dominic's illustration - wholesomely join in a winning stand celebratory of their amity.

The Go-between, possibly better known because of its faithful film and television versions and latterly as a musical, has Leo Colston, a visting youngster, acting as the innocent messenger in a clandestine and cross-class affair between Ted Burgess, a tenant farmer, and Marian Maudsley, daughter of the the lord of the manor and affianced to Lord Trimingham, who plays in the 'Hall' team. Called on to field Leo 'catches out' the impassioned farmer when he seems to be winning the game for the village, just as he unwittingly serves as the one who catches out Ted in his scandalous love-life. Ted blows out his brains (another case for David Frith?); Lord Trimingham, ever the toff, marries Marian and pretends to be the father of Ted's child by her, and Leo, in the hazily simmering heat of a pre-1914 summer is, in this Freudian referenced classic, traumatised sexually for life.

As well as these two excerpts there are several books that use the country house or village green game as an instalment within the whole, whereas there is one novel entirely devoted to rural cricket and this, too, has a definitive class component. This is Hugh de Selincourt's semi-autobiographical *The Cricket Match*, published in 1924. Hugh de Selincourt captained the West Sussex side of Storrington for seven years and this was the model for the fictitious Tillingfold club. Like two other books published about the same time, James Joyce's *Ulysses* (1922) and Virginia Woolf's *Mrs Galloway* (1925), the story occupies one single day.

J.M.Barrie, who showed a keen interest in cricket, declared this to be 'the best book written about cricket or any other game' while John Arlott wrote that 'one cricket novel stands high above the remainder...(as)...a fully realised novel.' Tillingfold is no idyllic hamlet with a duck pond and an oldest inhabitant. It has seven pubs and several shops; football and motor buses encroach and the team play their rivals Raveley on the recreation ground. Times they are a-changing. The characterisation is unforced and the writing shows great sensibility. There are generational and psychological variables as well as class distinctions, as Paul Gauvinier, an enlightened captain aka de Selincourt in flimsy disguise, leads his team to a thrilling but not over-dramatic two run victory. The class angle is carefully handled, with privileged Edgar Trine, son of the big house and Sid Smith the impoverished brick-layer and quick bowler able to join easily together as cricketers but experiencing discomfort as social animals. The social gradings of the players who fall between these two extremes are nuanced very neatly. As a portrait of recreational cricket, social strains, warts and all, in the period between the wars, it is both authentic and stylish.[7]

1. Wynne-Thomas op.cit. p. 150, See Simon Sweetman *Dimming of the Day; the Cricket Season of 1914* (2015) for an excellent analysis of the immediate effect of World War I on cricket nationally.
2. Gerald Howat *Cricket's Second Golden Age; the Hammond/Bradman Years* (1989).
3. Eric Midwinter 'The Profession of Gentlemen' *Cricket Lore* vol 1 issue 3 (1992).
4. Corelli Barnett *The Audit of War* (1986) and Martin Wiener *English Culture and the Decline of the Industrial Spirit* (1981) are recommended works on this topic.
5. Jack Williams *England and Cricket; a Cultural and Social History of the Inter-war Years* (1999) chap. 8 pp 161/182 on the financial issue; but this comprehensive and intently researched study is a major source for this period.
6. op.cit pp.59/60.
7. Eric Midwinter *Quill on Willow; Cricket in Literature* (2001) *passim* for these and other examples of literary treatments of cricket.

Chapter Ten
The Shadow Of Embourgeoisement

It was inevitable that, with top-class cricket more or less atrophied in the post-1918 years in a usually struggling economy, the professional cricketer's lot was not much happier in these decades than before 1914.

The counties made some early effort to compensate for the rising prices of 1914-1918 but little more was done before the onset of the second war. This was understandable in so far as prices steadied and then dropped in the 1930s. The composition of wages remained the same; a ground staff wage, match fees and possible talent money and a winter retainer, that last element a source of much debate among the county authorities. One sound development was the decision of the richer counties to declare a minimum annual guarantee of income for capped players, usually beginning at £200 but Surrey, often the most benevolent of the county employers, made £400 the bar and Lancashire £375.

A more typical county norm was a seasonal weekly wage of £3, home and away match fees of £8 and £10 respectively and a winter retainer of £2 a week, plus talent money of £1 for a fifty or a 'fifer'. In effect this meant that capped players received average annual earnings of £250 or £300. The usual qualification must be entered. They still had to provide their own flannels, boots and other equipment as well as travel and accommodation costs. Conversely, if they were lucky enough to find employment, they had seven clear months in which to earn extra money. Fitness and form were the key worries. A week out could mean the loss of £20 or thereabouts. Much is made today of the pressure on sportspersons of fabulous wealth. That would have sounded grimly comedic to the old-time cricket professional faced with not being able to make ends meet because he had a broken bone or a loss of form.[1]

The capped player's income of a weekly average of £5 or £6 did compare favourably with the upper tiers of the working classes, where a miner might earn £3 or £3.50 and an engine driver £5, and with the lower tiers of the middle classes, where clerks might be paid £2.10 to £7. In brief, a fifth of the work-force in the 1930s earned less than £2 a week, three-fifths between £2 and £5 and a fifth between £5 and £10, with a minority of that group on salaries higher than £10. To offer some perspective on those numbers, an average private or council rent or moderate mortgage payment would have been 5s to 8s a week.

Thus the mature pro retained his place among the proletarian elite. This only applied, of course, to the capped players, who made up approximately a third of the combined county ground staffs, something like 150 out of

350 professionals. The uncapped players, who may have been, needless to say, much younger men putting their toe gingerly into the water of a hoped for career, enjoyed no improvement in their pre-war conditions. Their all-round pay would have been £70 on £100 annually, close to that of an unskilled labourer or farm worker. It wasn't all bowling to members; there were all sorts of chores that might be heaped on the uncapped player between whom and the capped cricketer the gap had widened. Although one or two struggled on for some years in this capacity, it is probably more comprehensible to consider this group as and compared with apprentices, many of whom would soon fail to make the grade and drop out of the running.

At the opposite end of the cricketing trade another gap was opening. While, relatively, the unlucky non-capped ground staff members were falling behind, the stars were forging ahead. There were two reasons for this. On the one hand, their pay was enhanced and, on the other, celebrity brought them added income streams.

Test match fees started at £20 for the less popular series up to £40 for the Australians, plus bonuses. Rail travel was also covered. Those who played in all five Tests of the Australian rubber of 1930 received £250, the equivalent of the average professional's yearly pay. Moreover, Australian tours were most profitable. £400 was the going rate per player, with travel and accommodation excluded, unlike on the county circuit, and with high bonuses for successful trips approaching that same amount. However, there was, as usual, some ruefulness expressed over the fact that the amateur Australian tourists of 1930 received £600 for their cricketing pains.

Subscription lists for high performing English tourists and advertising opportunities for famous names also figured. There had been performer endorsement of cricket equipment in the past but now it expanded rapidly, with the fruitful addition of putting one's name to a non-cricketing product, such as Maurice Tate advertising Hovis bread and shredded wheat. Top players like Jack Hobbs or Ted McDonald had special contracts and, obviously enough, they tended to have more lucrative benefit matches. Jack Hobbs invested the £1671 from his delayed 1919 benefit in a sports business down Fleet Street which proved so profitable that he was a successful businessman while still playing. His annual earnings may well have been approaching £1500 at a time when the average income of a general practitioner was not much above £1000.[2] It was also easier for the stars to obtain winter work of a pleasant and undemanding sort such as sales of some kind, leaning heavily on their sporting reputation. A regular England professional could earn £800 in the year of an 'Australian' summer, something rather less in other seasons.

The benefit continued to play its part both in ensuring regular players had a little nest-egg at the termination of their employment with the counties while at the same time acting as an unspoken disciplinary goad against misconduct or undue complaining. The weather was but one of the variables which affected this end of career settlement yet it did ensure many cricketers found some monetary solace. George Hirst's record benefit of £3703 had been exceptional; it was a record that stood the test of time until 1925 when his fellow-Yorkshireman Roy Kilner collected £4016. Dovecotes fluttered in 1920 when the the £939 benefit of Kent's James Seymour was challenged by the Inland Revenue, arguing that this testimonial derived straightforwardly from the work he had done and was therefore subject to tax. It was a protracted case that wound itself through various court-rooms until ultimately it found itself in the House of Lords which ruled in favour of the beneficiary. Thus benefit proceeds were protected against taxation as long as they were patently in the form of 'a personal gift from the public.' Technically, this meant that a benefit could not be assured by being a condition of the player's contract; it had, notionally, to arise spontaneously through the gratitude of the fans.

The conventional comparison in respect of earnings is with association football. Cricket professionals were, on the whole, still better off than their footballing counterparts, always recalling that some – Denis Compton is a notable example – played both games professionally. In 1922 the maximum football weekly wage was actually reduced from £9 to £8, with £6 about the highest for the summer retainer. All this, amounting to £354 annually, applied only to a small fortunate or talented band, so with very few international add-ons, footballers did not do as well as capped cricketers overall. The registration system was very strict; a judicial decision in the 1913 case of Kingsby v Aston Villa went in favour of the club. The player claimed his livelihood had been lost because the club had hung too high a transfer fee upon him and he was no longer needed as an Aston Villa player. But the law of contract was upheld on the employer's side.

At least the footballers were not cursed with a restrictive birth or residential condition; not many Hotspurs were born in Tottenham. Furthermore, the range of opportunities was much wider. In the immediate post-war years two teams were added to the existing two divisions and two more divisions were added. Thus the mainline Football League was comprised of 92 clubs, with the Scottish Football League offering jobs to another series of clubs north of the border. Some of the stronger non-Football league competitions also employed some professional and many semi-professional players. In the Football League alone there must have been approaching 3000 paid players. Although the semi-professional genre and the many tales of back-handed payments to gifted amateurs created something of a grey area, football attempted, unlike cricket, to separate rather than combine the paid and unpaid player. The distinction continued to fall between the business-orientated professional spectator sport and the largely amateur recreational game. At this stage the Football Association had 10,000 clubs in affiliation and 750,000 young men and youths played football every weekend. During the 1930s the County FAs also took charge of schools football competitions and several thousand secondary schools were involved in these.

It was around the turn of the century that the annual numbers spectating at Football League fixtures passed those watching first-class cricket. By the inter-wars years, football was out-distancing cricket by millions. Compared with cricket's 1.5m or so a summer for first-class matches, the Football League's enlarged programme of forty or so games attracted approaching 1m every Saturday, with an average gate of 20,000. It will be recalled that 2000 paid what for some was a reluctant shilling to watch the first FA Cup Final. In 1923 Wembley Stadium was opened capable of holding 127,000 – and well over 200,000 overwhelmed the venue for the first Cup Final there.

This demonstrates the huge strides football had made in fifty years or so – and, incidentally, the good behaviour of the spectators on that first Wembley occasion is further testimony to Judith Flanders' succinct phrase 'the volatile mob had become the sedate consumer'.[3] A perplexed and astonished Irishman commented 'not a pistol went off' at a game played with 'human touchlines' preceded by a respectful rendition of the national anthem to greet George V.

The newspapers and the radio alike became very wedded to the football frenzy while an easily underestimated element in the spreading of this great interest was the football pools. Beginning in 1923 when 4000 pools coupons were distributed at Old Trafford football ground, by 1939 some £800,000 a week was being invested and there were 8m punters, representing a fifth of the adult population and two-thirds of the nation's households. Each week fifteen times as many as the huge crowds that attended the matches pored over the likely outcome of the fixtures and awaited the news of that outcome with some degree of concentration. It was a quantum leap in the penetration of the culture of the game among many who without the pools would not have known their Wolverhampton Wanderers from their West Bromwich Albions.

The ambuscade of cricket by football was very serious. In a relatively brief time and in a very business-like fashion the Football League and the FA had developed a simple, lucidly intelligible game with a concise time-frame and without undue vulnerability to inclement weather that was played as an entertainment in 92 outposts and with a great base of recreational engagement. Cricket had stood still and had been overtaken with ease. Horse racing remained the other rival for public involvement but this was a sport different in kind rather than degree. Many, high and low, followed it but betting – up to £200m annually at this juncture - was always the crux. Few 'played' it, for obvious reasons, nor was it in any way a team game nor a school or recreational pastime. Some might have a favourite jockey or horse but it did not engender the same sort of localised loyalty that characterised the league football or the county cricket club. Of course there was room for both cricket and football; it was more that cricket, trapped in the past, somehow missed the chance to fill the space that was available for it.

Cricket was no longer the 'national game' that once it had seemed to be. The Victorian charade, one part pleasant diversion, one part ethical exercise, had lost some of its gloss, although its leaders, against the logic of the mathematics, still claimed the high moral ground for a sport which, they asserted, was the essence of Englishry and by that token the distillation of moral probity. As late as the 1990s I found myself having a ding-dong row with a public school/Varsity blue England Test player who believed Oxford and Cambridge should enroll promising (male) cricketers with below par academic grades. His constant, indeed only, refrain was that cricket was 'the national game.'

In 1944 G.M.Trevelyan was to write his oft-cited quotation that 'if the French nobility had been capable of playing cricket, their chateaux would never have been burned.' This explication of the English class system being more benign and less caste-ridden than that of the French has been ceaselessly deployed by defenders of the cricketing faith. Trevelyan's critics would argue that, writing toward the encouraging later years of World War II and naturally optimistic in his Whig interpretation of unfailing progress, he may have erred on the sentimental side in this judgement. There is no doubt that cricket provided a locus for the coming together of the classes both as players and spectators and that this, in the natural way of things, contributed to the social calm. But it was more an effect than a cause, the cause being a much deeper and more extensive shift in social conditions. Nonetheless, Trevelyan's four volume story of English domestic life is brilliantly achieved.[4]

The point is that during this mid-wars era cricket could no longer assume, whatever the past devotion of its adherents, the degree of cultural and moral potency implicit in such statements. The relative serenity of late Victorian times was sustained. The cultural historian Jeffery Richards has developed the Victorian notion of the working classes being divided into self-explanatory 'respectable' and 'rough' categories. He suggests that before about the 1850s the rough element had been dominant and that thereafter and until after the Second World War the respectable component attained ascendancy, It might be argued as well that the middle and upper echelons of society also went through this switch of character. This syllogism is a valuable tool for a simple analysis of changing conditions and cultures. It is significant that, for cricket's two sequential 'Golden Ages', covering a hundred year cycle from the 1850s to the 1950s, the 'respectable' element was resolutely to the fore.[5]

Nevertheless, for all of cricket's petrified position between the two wars, there were straws in the wind. Even if the structure lay rigid, there were tiny movements in the superstructure that hinted at later more major changes. These clues lay in the borderland between the two classes. First of all, however, there was some levelling up to be done within the professional bracket itself. The nuances of a class-ridden society are numerous. There was a distinction between junior and senior staff, marked on some grounds, notably Lord's and the Oval, by separate dressing rooms, while, until counselled otherwise, the senior professional had to be addressed as 'sir' or 'mister'. Pettifogging although this may seem, one has to understand how in a tightly bonded group such conventions assumed telling significance.

The comparison with the army regiment with its Regimental Sergeant-major or domestic service with its butler very much in authoritative control is again self-evident. J.T.Hearne, when Middlesex's senior 'pro', ordered the time of meals and the time for going to bed. After first the seniors had sat down to eat and their juniors had shyly followed them to the chairs, he would enter, take over his place at the head of the table and preside over the repast. It could have been downstairs at Downton Abbey. It is unsurprising that the long-serving and immaculately mannered J.T.Hearne was, as early as 1902, invited to serve on the Middlesex Committee, the first professional anywhere so to be asked.[6] Ernest Tyldesley, the Lancashire and England batsman, who was considered at one time for the county captaincy, was another who served his club committee after his retirement in 1936. A sedate and thoughtful man, he would not have made waves and would have offered his opinions quietly and sparingly.

This all eased a little as the years drew by but the amateur/professional barriers were mainly retained. Some counties did not have separate dressing rooms by this time, although amateur captains who essayed to lead out their troops through one gate at Lord's received short shrift. During this era, in part owing to the decline in the number of amateurs available, a number of professionals, some two dozen, captained their counties on occasion. Jack Hobbs, who was to shatter the mould with his knighthood long after he had retired in 1953, was always reluctant to step into the captaincy shoes either with England or Surrey; even when a knighted elder he was wont to embarrass callow young amateurs by addressing them as 'sir or 'mister'. Alf Gover, the Surrey fast bowler, has recorded both the church-going Jack Hobbs's severe intolerance of bad language in the dressing room and of his own embarrassment when, on becoming a senior, he found it acutely painful to mumble 'Jack' instead of Mr Hobbs.

Ewart Astill was the first professional actually to be appointed a county captain. He skippered Leicestershire in 1935 in what was one of their most satisfying campaigns but his appointment was not renewed and Leicestershire slumped again. Ewart Astill, a highly consistent all-rounder, was a capable man who, unusually for a paid cricketer, had gained a commission with the Machine Gun Corps in World War1, but somehow the Leicester committee was not tempted to reappoint him.

On the other side, there were amateurs who verged on a genuine if slightly glossed over professionalism of a kind which even the most cynical 'player' did not feel breached the code of 'gentleman'. This was where the captain acted also as what now would be called the chief executive of the club, the head cook and bottle-washer who made it his career to keep the county in workable condition. These were not the sinecures of the purported 'assistant secretaries', masks to fund young amateurs; these were full-time gruelling jobs. The chief example in these pre-1939 days was Maurice Turnbull at Glamorgan; he ruefully complained how he wore his feet out dancing at fund-raising balls and altogether did a most efficacious job for that hitherto ailing county. Two other instances were Cyril Walters and Vallance Jupp at Worcestershire and and Northants respectively. That captain-cum-secretary was the sort of role undertaken by Trevor Bailey at

Essex in the post-war years.[6]

Although grammar schools were and remained a largely middle-class preserve, some of their products, having graced their school first elevens, found employment as first-class cricketers, among them Leslie Ames, the Kent and England wicket keeper-batsman, of Harvey Grammar School, Folkstone, George Cox Junior whose father was also a Sussex professional, of Collier's Grammar School, Horsham and Cyril Washbrook, the Lancashire and England opener, of Bridgnorth Grammar School. In all these and like cases their family background was of a middling grade where there was some ambition for the gifted son to do well, in Cyril Washbrook's case the hope that he would go on to university. Here again we observe paid cricketers coming from a sometimes indefinable shaded area between the overt industrial working class and the patently professional middle class families. On the other hand, George Duckworth, the Lancashire and England wicketkeeper, was a clever child from a poorer home who won a scholarship to the Boteler Grammar School in Warrington but had to leave after three years owing to family money pressures. His potential was demonstrated not just in his superb wicket keeping and trademark appeal but in his magnificent achievements as an administrator and organiser during and just after the Second World War.[7]

There is no doubt that the involvement of cricketers of this ilk, although for the most part they obeyed with admirable decorum the conventions of the split class world they inhabited, signalled the changes ahead. In this narrative of professional improvement and identity two very talented cricketers stood out. One was Herbert Sutcliffe and one was Wally Hammond. They were destined to give professional cricketers a very encouraging boost in their self-regard, the former almost as some form of personal crusade, the latter more by the trajectory of his career.

Where Jack Hobbs was dignified and peacefully deferential, his partner and friend in perhaps the most successful opening partnership in Test cricket was determinedly aspirational. Herbert Sutcliffe was a remarkably self-confident man, regarded with awe by the likes of Len Hutton, and no wonder. His origins were disadvantaged. Orphaned as a youngster, he was brought up by an aunt in Pudsey and apprenticed as a 'clicker', a fastener of soles to uppers in the manufacture of boots and shoes. He quickly escaped to clerical work and cricketing duties, then along came the First World War. He soon became a corporal in the Sherwood Foresters stationed at York but then was commissioned as a second lieutenant with The Green Howards at Salisbury. Perhaps this crossing of the class lines was the most amazing fact of his intriguing life. He was not a first-class cricketer at this point, for he made his debut for Yorkshire in 1919. His future partner was in wartime air mechanic Jack Hobbs.

Once established as a leading player, he made it his business to outdo the amateur. This was not part of some left-wing insurgency. He was not interested in creating, for instance, a militant trade union or syndicate. He once scolded his team-mate and admirer Bill Bowes, the Yorkshire and England quick bowler, for not wearing his blazer to lunch. Bill Bowes had left his blazer in the dressing room because his amateur skipper had done so but Herbert Sutcliffe severely instructed him, 'we must do everything better than the amateurs. Your manners must be better, and if possible you must speak and dress better, too.'[8] His aim, therefore, was not to make a proud trade with a craft guild character like an engineers' or electricians' union. His aim was to make cricket a profession in the style of teaching or medicine or law.

He was certainly triumphant in terms of himself in this regard. Rising to be a major in World War II, he built a flourishing sports outfitting business in Leeds and Wakefield, which his son took over in the post-war years. Herbert Sutcliffe then became a representative and later a director of a paper manufacturing business where – most exquisite of ironies – his former England captain, Douglas Jardine, haughtiest of leaders, was employed as company secretary. He sent his son William Herbert Hobbs Sutcliffe to Rydal School; rejoicing in that glorious trio of initials, he played for Yorkshire as an amateur and captained the club in 1956 and 1957. Herbert Sutcliffe's immediate famed predecessors with Yorkshire and England, Wilfred Rhodes and George Hirst had coached at such schools, the one at Harrow, the other at Eton. Now a fellow-professional ushered his son into a public school and, later, Len Hutton would emulate his guru by packing off his son Richard to Repton, prior to his cricketing days with Cambridge University, Yorkshire and England.[9]

Thus began the gentrification of the English cricket professional. Thus started his transformation into a middle class typology of professional. Wally Hammond, whose claim to be one of cricket's premier batsmen is non-negotiable, was also a leading light on the social as well as the sporting front. Rather like W.G.Grace, he found himself falling between two class stools and it is apparent that, as he matured, this confused him and left him discontented. His father was a regular soldier who, in the tumult of the 1914-18 conflict, shot up through the ranks to become a major. He was killed in 1918. His widowed mother managed on a relatively small income to educate her son at Portsmouth Grammar School as a day boy and Cirencester Grammar School as a boarder, hopeful that he would take up farming. Thereafter he became a Gloucestershire professional; there was certainly no family money to fund him as an amateur.

Wally Hammond was also a gifted enough footballer with Plymouth Argyle and Bristol Rovers to evoke prophecies of him being a double international. His reluctance to continue as a professional footballer like several other cricketers such as Harry Makepeace (Everton and England) and Andy Ducat (Aston Villa and England) gives rise to two compelling points. One is that he believed, rightly, that, as a paid cricketer, with the promise of overseas tours, he would be able to afford a small car and maybe even purchase a modest home, neither of which was possible for the lower paid footballer. But his perceptive biographer, Gerald Howat, makes an even more telling point in describing Wally Hammond's distaste for the plebeian ethos of professional football: 'the football world was more proletarian than he cared for. He was a little different from the rest of the Bristol Rovers squad.'[10]

He developed a mode of life more in keeping with a 'gentleman'. His two marriages – to Dorothy Lister from a wealthy Bradford textile family and to Sybil Ness-Harvey from a moneyed South African background – were definitively upwardly mobile. During the Second World War he became a squadron-leader in the RAF, commissioned like others of his England colleagues such as Leslie Ames, Bill Edrich and Hedley Verity. Herbert Sutcliffe was sure to have noted with quiet approval Bill Bowes's commission as a gunnery officer. However, before this Walter Hammond made the major breakthrough of becoming an amateur and captaining England. In 1937, to be more specifically accurate, he became a 'gentleman', courtesy of a £2000 *per annum* directorship with the Marsham Tyres Company with permission, indeed encouragement, to play cricket whenever required. Doubtless he earned some of this corn through the use of his name and presence in terms of sales, but it was in reality a spectacular species of Shamateurism. It was almost four times his earnings as a paid cricketer and it was nearly eight times as much as the captain of the English football team, Eddie Hapgood, the stylish Arsenal full-back, was paid. The whole strategy had obviously been vetted, approved and perhaps even instigated by some of the cricketing authorities. They preferred to switch the class of the man rather than offend the code of the class.

Nonetheless, the integrated class culture that permitted such a degree of social mobility was not to everybody's satisfaction. Hobnobbing and fraternisation was one thing but transference was another. The unease it caused was voiced on behalf of the more conservative faction by Neville Cardus. He was disconcerted by Wally Hammond and Herbert Sutcliffe wearing Savile Row suits and generally parading like top executives, with the latter speaking 'not with the accents of Yorkshire but of Teddington.' Neville Cardus, watching with alarmed disgust the possible change in the models of wry crustiness he had utilised for his eloquent descriptions, may himself have had a professional axe to grind. The estimable, envy-free, knowledgeable northern 'player' had served his copy well. It was as if L.S.Lowry's matchstick men had suddenly straightened up, bought city-style bowlers and umbrellas and started reading the *Daily Telegraph*. 'The county cricketer in certain instances', Neville Cardus gloomily wrote, 'has become a man of bourgeois profession'.[11]

The use of the adjective 'bourgeois' is instructive, for, in effect, cricketers like Wally Hammond and Herbert Sutcliffe were undergoing what in the 1960s would be called embourgeoisement. In those pre-war days they might have been described as absorbing suburban values. Over against the dark clouds of the slump in the heavy manufacturing areas, the bright sunshine of a growing suburbia was to be observed. Ribbon development of semi-detached residences, Metroland, 'Baby' Austins, trim lawns and hedges, 'table ready' foodstuffs, 'the religion of home improvement', vacuum cleaners (sales of which went up from 18,000 in 1930 to 410,000 in 1935): these components and others contributed to the suburban dream. One would like to believe that Emmie Sutcliffe and Sybil Hammond had vacuum cleaners – and possibly even domestic servants to operate them. Apparently Herbert Sutcliffe, Bill Bowes, Hedley Verity and Len Hutton became Freemasons, very far removed from the friendly societies associated with the working classes.[12]

Of course, only a handful of paid cricketers had the self-confidence and the high ability to enjoy such self-improvement while some, more in the wake of Jack Hobbs, might have preferred a less stressful social battle. Herbert Sutcliffe is said to have been disappointed when his close friend Jack Hobbs resisted essays to engage in captaincy at the top level. Perhaps someone like George Duckworth, who had an eminently worthy post-playing career without losing or seeking to lose his formative roots and values, is an example of a professional cricketer who was at ease in his own skin, never seeking to exalt himself.

Nevertheless, this upmarketing of professional cricket, with Walter Hammond and Herbert Sutcliffe the indisputable pioneers, may be judged in hindsight as the most salient alteration in the mainly changeless construct of cricket between the two wars. Taking a lateral glance at other sports, they were in the good company of sporting heroes such as Henry Cotton, Gordon Richards and Fred Perry who, in very differing fashions in the same era, were putting a similar imprint on their sport, as they struggled to come to terms with the class-ridden nature of golf, of racing and of lawn tennis.

1. Sissons op.cit where these issues are exhaustively discussed, especially chap. 9 'A Sense of Security' pp.193/221.
2. John Arlott *Jack Hobbs* (1981) for this and other details of Jack Hobbs's quite handsome living.
3. Flanders op, cit.
4. G.M.Trevelyan *English Social History* (1944).
5. Jeffrey Richards *Films and British National Identity; from Dickens to Dad's Army* (1997) is one of a number of this author's references to the 'respectable' and 'rough' phenomenon.
6. Sissons op.cit. pp.242/52 for much of the foregoing paragraphs.
7. Eric Midwinter *George Duckworth; Warrington's Ambassador at Large* (2007).
8. Bill Bowes *Express Deliveries* (1949).
9. Alan Hill *Herbert Sutcliffe; Cricket Maestro* (1991) for probably the best account of the Yorkshire star's life.
10. Gerald Howat *Walter Hammond* (1984) – this is one of the finest of cricket biographies.
11. Christopher Brookes *Neville Cardus; His Own Man* (1985) for the most succinct account of his varied life and substantial influence.
12. Mark Rowe '*Swearing in Brian Sellers' Time at Yorkshire County Cricket Club 1932-71' The Cricket Statistician* issue no 176 winter 2016, itself an interesting discourse on the cross-class nature of masculine foul language.

Chapter Eleven
Cricket and Society in the 1940s

We have a Tolstoyan 'war and peace' view of the 1940s; 1945 acts as a vast watershed in the popular mind. Although it would be callously wayward to forget the distress and suffering of the war years, there was, domestically, something of a continuum. Ten or so years of a Collectivist structure and mind-set made for a more complete decade on the home front. In brief, it was a combine of what has been called 'War Socialism' and 'the Silent Revolution' of 1945/51.

Britain handed itself over to its government lock, stock and barrel, with the central statute of the 1939 Emergency Powers (Defence) Act ensuring a comprehensive range of control over lives, property and material. The Civil Service doubled to 700,000 and much of this officialdom was retained post-war. Wearing and tedious as this often was, the public was supportive of the war aims and kept a strong sense of social stability. A.J.P.Taylor's kind but correct opinion was that 'the British people came of age...tolerant, patient and generous'.[1]

If one may select a cricketing metaphor, Britain emerged as one of the victors having lost heavily on the first innings. From a morale viewpoint, and compared with the enemy, matters improved as the war drew on. The United Kingdom was the only European combatant country not occupied and in part destroyed by a foe. Aside from the brief if hideous V1 and V2 rockets afflicting the London area late in the war, the major bombing was over by late 1941 with many areas scarcely affected. There was a dissonance between expectation and actuality. The official forecast had been that there would be 600,000 dead blitz victims in the first two months of the war, whereas the total for the entire conflict was 51,000 civilian deaths. To put that in context, Germany suffered 1.5m civilian deaths, while in a mere eleven weeks in 1944 from D-Day to the Liberation of Paris, 70,000 French civilians were killed by bombing and bombardment.

In this relatively pacific clime, the chief upbeat common denominator for the decade was full employment. There was still an overhang from the depression of 1m out of work in 1939 - but by the end of 1940 everyone had a job, the beginning of what was to be the only lengthy period of full employment in British economic history. It has been statistically shown that during these years Britain was the most efficiently organised and productive industrial state ever known. This deliberate essay in public ownership, social welfare and fiscal severity was sustained after the war during the Labour Government's time in office, Planning was the key. It was frequently said in so many words that we had planned for a well-earned victory and now we must plan for a worthwhile peace. A people inured to the Collectivist habits and practices of three generations took the more easily to both the demands of total war and then post-war regeneration. The distinguished historian Ian Kershaw recently wrote 'Britain was quite possibly a society more united during the war than it had ever been before or would be again.[2]

The 'fair shares for all' mantra, like the expectation that everyone would 'do his or her bit', makes for a succinct descriptor of this mood. Rationing was popularly welcomed, even demanded. Careful nutritional standards were well managed and extreme shortages avoided. Interestingly, the sales of bacon and butter soared because before joblessness fell and wages rose, these had been luxuries for many families, while government subsidies kept down the price of essential foodstuffs. The Briton out-caloried the German by 2400 calories a day to 2000; indeed, that British total was higher than the average pre-war intake. Furthermore, the consumption of calories and proteins levelled out between the working and middle classes, adding culinary to cultural integration. And rationing, of course, was maintained throughout the decade and into the early 1950s.

The Welfare State itself, far from being in the fevered political minds of the late 20th century either the crimson glory of Socialism or what its acidic critic F.A. Hayek called 'the Road to Serfdom', had a quite benign derivation.[3] The phrase the Welfare State was coined by an Oxford academic Alfred Zimmern in 1934 and popularised by William Temple, Archbishop of Canterbury; it was a counterweight to the 'Warfare State' at a time when both Fascist and Soviet totalitarian regimes were mocking parliamentary government for its feebleness in coping with the great depression.

The amount of social care and medical service increased manifold during the war building on the reforms of the late Victorian and Edwardian periods, with the formulation of a uniform system, with the National Health Service pivotal, more a consolidation than a reformation. Its progenitor William Beveridge saw it all in patriotic terms, believing that the universalism of welfare was, in the words of his biographer Jose Harris, 'desirable to foster social solidarity and feelings of identification.'[4] This sentiment of a unified people joining as one to fight a military enemy abroad and then a social enemy at home was a strong and durable one.[5]

Fiscally, the crisis of war and the needs of peace alike resulted in high taxation, with usually a standard income tax rate of 50% and a top rate of 97.5% plus very high Purchase Tax on luxury goods. Throughout the 1940s the tax system was intently redistributive, with a high threshold before tax began and heavy subsidies of staple foods and social care. The nation was more egalitarian than at any time before or since. By 1951 the top rich 1% had watched aghast as its share of national wealth had fallen from 22% in 1914 to 10%. There were only 60 people in the country with more than £6000 a year to spend out of income.[6]

What has been perhaps underrated in past studies has been the 1940s continuum in terms of domestic governance. While Winston Churchill brilliantly and valorously negotiated the tribulations of a terrible war, he consigned much of the running of the home front to his Deputy Prime Minister, Clement Attlee, the Labour leader with whom the premier had a sound and trusty working relationship. Clement Attlee's two chief adjutants were both Labour comrades-in-arms, namely, Herbert Morrison, Home Secretary and Minister for Home Security and Ernest Bevin, Minister of Labour. This trio then formed the core of the 1945-51 Labour Government. In effect, Clement Attlee was in charge of the internal running of the United Kingdom from 1940, when the wartime coalition was formed, until 1951, when the Labour administration fell narrowly at the polls.

Public order remained at its high level. Crime continued at an abnormally low rate by international criteria. In a recent study of the black market in all combatant nations in World War II the United Kingdom emerged as the least troubled. Such good conduct played itself out in the arena of leisure. A curio of the times is that expenditure on leisure between 1938 and 1944 increased by 120% and continued upwards in the post-war years. This was in consequence of full employment and improved wages which in real terms rose by 50%. This was the heyday of the cinema – 30m cinema tickets sold each week; 1.5bn a year; 75% of the adult population were film-goers – while the variety theatre was still active and lively. The dance halls attracted 4m customers a week, that is 200m a year; it has been estimated that 70% of married couples at this time met on the dance floor. Football League attendances amounted to 90m annually in the post-war years, although the truncated and regional wartime competitions also attracted great hosts. The queue was the social symbol of the age. There were vast crowds but they behaved, on the whole, patiently.

The counterpart in the home was the radio. In spite of, probably because of, its narrowness of content, its appeal was, paradoxically broad. In 1923 200,000 licences were bought; by the early 1930s sales had risen to 5m; in 1939 nine out of ten households had licenses. It peaked in 1948 with 8.8m. Writing about the history of the BBC in 2014 Charlotte Higgins pointed out that it was 'the first time...a physically dispersed general public had been able to experience events simultaneously'. Over 20m people tuning in to Tommy Handley's *ITMA* or Wilfred Pickles' *Have a Go* were genuinely defining moments of collective enjoyment.

Cricket was an early beneficiary. In 1927 the BBC had begun its lengthy series of ball-by-ball commentaries, with, after a rocky start, sizable audiences tuning in from all parts and social sectors of the country, The soothing tones of Howard Marshall soon became almost as recognisable as those, say, of Uncle Mac, Donald McCulloch, the long-time host and Toytown's Larry the Lamb of *Children's Hour*. In these later years post-war, of course, John Arlott's superlative gifts placed him in the pantheon not just of great sports commentators but of all eminent British broadcasters. The 'wireless' seemed to lend itself to the slower rhythm of cricket, a game where meditative appreciation was the keynote.

All in all, the 1940s witnessed the point where the cultural integration of the artisan and suburban classes touched closest to a social union. It was the culmination of a hundred years of this process. The word 'middlebrow' had been coined by the magazine *Punch* in 1910 and, apposite as it already then was, it was in the 1940s decade that the word most closely defined the habits and moods of the British public. The American academic Martin Reiner wrote 'the English way of reconciling respect for individual liberty with a very high degree of public order and cooperation was the envy of the world'.[7]

A detailed disquisition on the 1940s is a necessary preliminary to an account of cricket's fortunes in that important decade, for it is arguable that this phase marked the game's finest but final years as a broadly based and deeply embedded sport, nationally acknowledged and appreciated.

The attitude towards cricket in the Second was the converse of what it had been in the First of the World Wars. It was recognised that in the grim attrition of total war both military and civilian personnel had the need of relief and respite. Importantly, there was also the fund-raising component; a lot of the matches played were in aid of war charities. There was also a propaganda element; it was recognised that stopping cricket at Lord's would have been a *coup* for Joseph Goebbels, the expert if satanic Nazi communicator.

Proposals to run some kind of county competition, perhaps on a regional basis, were denied. Although, perhaps mistakenly, the cricketing powers ruled out any such official attempt, unlike the Football League who contrived so to do, there was encouragement to those who wished to organise and play the game. In the event, and increasingly, the amount of cricket played was substantial at all levels. As until the closing stages of the war none of it was first-class, its impact has perhaps been underestimated.

This *laissez-faire* or, to use a 1940s phrase, 'go as you please' approach meant there was a mixture of cricketing opportunities both at playing and spectating levels. For example, there was a considerable degree of forces' cricket and also among the civil defence personnel, with fire service, wardens, home guards and so on forming teams. Some counties tried to sustain a fixture list while Lord's planned an excellent programme, often with military connotations, for which Sir Pelham Warner was largely responsible. Two interesting developments were the British Empire XI, a strictly amateur outfit, and the London Counties XI, just as sternly professional, keen to preserve cricketing standards and protect the income of players unfit for military service. Throughout the war these two elevens played well over 400 fixtures. League cricket was maintained in the war years, with professional engagements increasing in the latter years of hostilities. In the north-west the prolixly titled Lady Kemsley's *Daily Dispatch* War Fund XI was a staple. Under the masterly oversight of George Duckworth they played reinforced local clubs on every Sunday throughout every season of the war.

Two significant points arise from this motley display of cricketing persistence in the face of war. The first concerns the incidence of the activity and the way in which famous names would be seen playing on ordinary club pitches. The cricket was more recreational than competitive in style, for entertainment was the *motif* but there were myriad chances to see one's heroes at close quarters rather than secreted away in just seventeen shire bases out of reach of many. For six summers there were regular appearances of well-known English and also West Indian and, especially in the later years of the conflict, Australian and other Dominions players widely across the country. For instance, in the flourishing Bradford League spectators might have watched up to five well-known first-class cricketers every Saturday. Not since the long ago era of the Exhibition elevens had there been so comprehensive a spread of high-class talent.

The second point is even more salient. The crowds that turned out to watch these games were amazingly large. Even in the worrying summer of 1940 the British Empire XI attracted over 80,000 to its 37 matches, an average of more than 2000 a game. Another example was the work of A.D.Procter in the north-west. As head of the Welfare Section of the Ministry of Labour and National Service in Manchester it was his task to raise funds for welfare scheme. Cricket was his chosen mode. In 1942, for instance, he arranged a score or more matches which drew average crowds of 5000, reaching a total of 125,000.

Similar matches were happening all over the country. Warwickshire, after an uneasy start to the war including war damage to Edgbaston, extended its wings until in 1945 it arranged a fixture list second only to Lord's. The highlight was a Festival week, with an attractive one day fixture every day as part of the Birmingham 'Holidays at Home' programme. The 1945 event was the fourth annual festival in the series which welcomed 150,000 in total to Edgbaston.

Nottinghamshire's experiences make for lively comparison. Only twice in the 1939 season did paying customers (that is, excluding members) exceed 2000 and they were occasionally as small as a hundred or so. Under the energetic leadership of the club secretary H.A.Brown, Notts organised an ambitious list of weekend matches throughout the hostilities with the following results in respect of attendance: 1940, 7 games 6000; 1941, 8 games 6100; 1942, 7 games (two days lost to rain) 5000; 1943, 8 games 9000; 1944, 8 games (one day lost to rain) 19,000 and 1945, 11 games 27,000, including one crowd of 7000. The average gate in 1944 and 1945 was 2300.

Not surprisingly, as the trajectory of the Trent Bridge figures show, the gates grew as the war situation at home eased, reaching a bustling culmination in the summer of 1945. *Wisden* reports some 270 games for that season, including eleven declared first-class, among them the five much celebrated Victory Tests and another 24 two-day matches. According to Sir Pelham Warner the exhilarating occasion of the England and Dominions fixture in which 1241 runs were scored was 'one of the finest matches played at Lord's'. There were over thirty days cricket at Lord's in 1945. The total attendance over the summer was an astounding 414,000, an average of over 12,000 a day, with the gates locked four times.

This compared favourably with the 330,000 of 1939 when some 60 days cricket were each watched by an average of 5500. Huge crowds up and down the country told the same story.

Did the authorities read any lessons into the fact that a programme knocked together by different enthusiasts up and down the nation had proved more popular than the staid ritual of the county championship? Reconstruction was the keyword on post-war lips. In many areas from broadcasting and housing to aeronautics and medicine, there were positive plans and immediate action by way of reform and improvement. Would cricket sign up for progress?

It certainly went through the motions. All kinds of suggestions were proffered. In 1942/43 the Advisory County Cricket Committee and then a Select Committee of the same met to decide on the construct of post-war cricket. It was one of those junctures when the oligarchic as opposed to the democratic aspects of cricket made the judgements. The long-established settlement of the cross-class concord was not observed. Those wartime spectators, by token of their numbers primarily working and lower middle class in status, had voted with their shillings for an updated, more exciting sort of cricket. Their masters thought otherwise. The moderate plan for a two-day cricket based on weekend and half-day closing days, with counties playing one another home and away, plus a strong incentive to provide more entertaining cricket was almost contemptuously rejected. There were memories of the two-day matches of the 1919 season which had not been a wholly satisfactory experiment. There were other recommendations, including proposals to end the 'surely humbug' of the amateur/professional distinction and others to promote divisions, the amalgamation of counties, a knock-out competition and Sunday cricket. Virtually none was adopted.

Dynamic captaincy, implicitly by amateurs, was the answer, otherwise there was no need for basic change. 'I can see nothing wrong with modern cricket' said Sir Pelham Warner, stalwart protagonist of wartime cricket but so much more at heart the steady keeper of the fort rather than the imaginative explorer of its hinterland. The one innings version, long practised at the recreational and league level, was barely discussed; it was 'just a jolly wartime expedient'. R.C.Robertson-Glasgow was most scathing. He called one day cricket 'the new clockwork monkey in the nursery' while three day cricket was 'a three-act play not a slapstick turn' and for those who were ignorant enough to think otherwise, 'such spectators are, frankly, not wanted at county cricket'. Not immediately but in a year or so, they took him at his word.[8]

A gloss on the decision to oppose change was the persistence in a belief that cricket had a special, even sacred, aura, rendering alteration from the ritual of the three-day county game something close to blasphemy. In fairness to the cricketing elite who opted for this immaculate system, the popularity of first-class cricket for the first few post-war seasons gave rise to a reasonable complacency that all boded well.

Cricket buffs are possibly better versed in these years than in the more complex skein of wartime cricket. A damp 1946 brought a courteous if slightly disorientated Indian touring side to these war-torn shores and all the counties managed to break even financially. 1947 was a bonanza summer. 3m flocked through the turnstiles or, as members, hurried to the pavilions, a busy matter of 10,000 a day, as, in mainly glorious sunshine, Denis Compton and Bill Edrich shattered batting records in Middlesex's famous championship triumph. Kent attracted 200,000 paying spectators; twice as many as in 1939. 1948 was a another good year for the county treasurers, if less so for the county coaches as Don Bradman's Invincibles conquered all before them in a devastating sweep through the kingdom.[9]

Meanwhile, there were preliminary clues of the internal changes that were occurring whether the authorities liked them or not. There was a packed house at Old Trafford for the first day of Lancashire's game against the visiting Australians of 1948. Against all previous practice, the Lancashire committee had kindly favoured Cyril Washbrook with this fixture for his benefit match. It was also the first benefit venture to have the services of its own special committee who organised a season-long series of fund-raising Sunday matches and other events, all of which endeavour resulted in a spectacular sum of over £14,000 for the fortunate Lancashire hero. It was a record amount that stood the test of time.

During the interval Cyril Washbrook spoke of his appreciation to the crowd over the public address system, that mechanism itself being something of a novelty. These, it must be remembered, were more humane times when sports personalities were not supposed to have the conversational powers of a Max Beerbohm or an Oscar Wilde in addition to their footballing or cricketing skills. In other words, we were not used then to hearing them speak. Today, cruelly, on radio and, worse, on television, all players are forced orally to display their leaden modesty and despairing cliches, to their embarrassment and to the discomfort of the sensitive listener or watcher. As soon as Cyril Washbrook opened his mouth a reactive murmur ran through the throng. He spoke in assured, deep, unaccented tones. It was not the voice we had expected to emanate from the larynx of a Lancashire professional. We had not thought it would be all 'ee bah gum ' dialect but we were surprised it was not more homely and broad-vowelled in intonation. I have a very clear remembrance of my own teen-age response – which was that he spoke like a teacher.

A horrified Neville Cardus and a gratified Herbert Sutcliffe would have alike acknowledged that change was afoot. World War II saw a shake-up of the social conventions. They were in succession to the pre-war hints of a suburban, even bourgeois, cut of the professional cricketer's jib. Another of these portents, one referred to earlier, was the number of professional cricketers commissioned in World War II in marked difference to its rarity in World War I. Major Sutcliffe and Squadron Leader Wally Hammond have already been mentioned in dispatches. Army colleagues of the former to be commissioned were, among others, Hedley Verity, Stan Worthington, Bill Bowes, Alf Gover and Maurice Leyland, while the latter's fellow RAF officers included Bill Edrich and Leslie Ames. Wally Hammond, of course, had turned amateur shortly before and Bill Edrich followed suit shortly after the war.

Hedley Verity died, sadly, of his wounds and Bill Bowes had a long spell in a prisoner of war camp. Bill Edrich lived, as he has vividly described, a strangely split life of heroic aerial feats one day and cricketing jaunts the next. But for some of the ex-officers and indeed senior non-commissioned officers, such as RAF sergeants Washbrook and Hutton, the latter invalided out with an arm injury in 1942, must have felt that the return to the status and income of a professional cricketer was something of a backward step, even given the relief from the anxiety of war.

Both cricket and football authorities sought to retain the wage levels of yesteryear but the professionals in both sports knew full well that gate receipts had been fruitful in the later war years and that manufacturing wages had doubled. The Professional Footballer Association posed the threat of a strike and a deal was briskly cut in 1946 of a weekly £10 maximum throughout the season and a £7.10 summer retainer, an overall rise approaching 25%. The cricket authorities had hoped that the £440 maximum of 1939 would suffice but, as the usual round of county by county negotiations began before the 1946 season, there was considerable leverage to improve on this,

Surrey and Lancashire, the two leading counties in terms of the remuneration on offer, consulted closely with representatives of the playing staff. As before, the gradings remained quite complex but, in summary, an established Surrey first eleven professional earned £500 to £550 (with a guarantee of £450) annually in those immediate post-war years and their Lancashire coevals a little more, perhaps as much as £600 (£416 guaranteed). This very roughly represented something like a 25% increase on pre-war levels of pay. The poorer counties could not match that degree of generosity but all felt obliged to improve on their pre-war wage packets in some proportionate fashion. For the international elite there were slightly richer pickings. Players chosen for the 1946-47 Australian tour received £550, a 60% increase on 1930s trips, plus expenses and a possible bonus of up to £275, but they netted only £450, and no expenses, for the South African tour of 1948-49.[10]

English professionals received £75 for a home Test match and that was the standard rate for some time. In private conversation with Brian Statham he explained to me how Fred Trueman and he lost money as internationals. In the 1950s both Lancashire and Yorkshire paid their top-grade capped players a generous match fee of £50. Test duties often meant that these two world-class figures missed two matches per Test, so that in a five fixture rubber they were down a probable £125 on the overall deal.

Brian Statham was extraordinary in his ordinariness; it is inconceivable that a man could have risen to such heights of international sporting fame and remained completely untouched or untarnished by the experience. Sitting together on the Lancashire committee balcony one afternoon, Brian

Statham told me the story of his initial first-class wicket. It is well-known that he came to cricket relatively late when spotted bowling during his national service by the eagle-eyed RAF Corporal Lazarus. Until Lancashire took an interest in him, he had never visited Old Trafford and he was drafted into the first eleven very rapidly. He made his debut at Old Trafford against Kent in 1950 and the authoritarian Cyril Washbrook, the county's senior professional, sternly advised him not to bowl short to the Kent opener Arthur Fagg, a man reputed to be a ferocious hooker. In his second over Brian Statham did bowl a short ball and Arthur Fagg, perhaps surprised by the kind of pace that was very scarce on the county circuit in those years, mistimed his hook and was caught at forward short leg.

Today a prized wicket, let alone the first in someone's career, would lead to a near-hysterical festival of triumphant high fives, man-hugs and back-slaps. Professional cricketers were made of tougher fibre then. Cyril Washbrook stormed up to the errant bowler and scolded him. 'Statham, I told you not to bowl short to Arthur Fagg.' Even as a twenty-year old tyro, the fast bowler was his own man, quiet but obdurately independent. 'No', he replied, 'but then you didn't tell me which one was Arthur Fagg....and, while we're on the subject, I don't know the names of half the bloody Lancashire team.' That succinct cameo has something to say about the mood of the professional game then; the classroom or barrack square usage of the surname by the autocratic senior; the reprimand for disobedience rather than the good cheer over a wicket taken if accidentally; the impoverished induction of the new recruit into the squad... Happily the new recruit on this occasion turned out into a highly skilled sharpshooter; Fred Trueman is not the only good judge to assert that 'George', as Statham was known in the Lancashire dressing room in succession to Winston Place, was the most accurate fast bowler in cricket history.

A rightful governmental edict ensured that former workers returning from military duties or war work must be re-employed, which, given the wartime Direction of Labour statute, meant practically everybody. Thus the 1946 county elevens looked suspiciously like the 1939 one, a factor, incidentally, in the popularity of cricket in those immediate post-war seasons. Lots of fans wanted a last look at their pre-war cigarette card heroes. These veterans also masked a fault-line in the production of young cricketers. Almost a hundred young cricketers made their debut in the 1946 summer but few lasted the pace.

Although much has been made, and rightly so, of the records that would have been broken had the likes of Wally Hammond, Denis Compton, Len Hutton, to say nothing of Don Bradman, played first-class cricket in all those lost seasons, what has been often forgotten is the six year hiatus in any sort of nursery for or nurture of fledgling first-class cricketers. This problem is underpinned by the statistics. In the central phase of 1915/1930, when those born then would have been, say, 24 to nineteen in 1939, the births of English first-class cricketers drops below an average of 20 a year, whereas in the fore and aft eras of 1905/1915 and 1930/35 the figure is over 30. The veterans were sorely required. It was the Trueman/

Statham/Tyson vintage of around 1930 who provided the next genuine supply of English cricketing cream, even if Tom Graveney, Jim Laker and Godfrey Evans were among the outstanding exceptions that prove that generational rule.

The counter attraction of better paid jobs in the manufacturing industries and elsewhere posed a threat to the flow of professional players, £7.50/£8 a week, £350 a year, was by now the norm for skilled tradesmen. Work in engineering or light industries was not suddenly curtailed nor, in an epoch of full employment and sturdy trades unionism, subject to the equivalent of the whim of an umpire's faulty LBW decision or an inconvenient injury.

As the post-war settlement matured, there was, in relative terms, a high level of social mobility. Social mobility is a much abused phrase. However, as an integral aspect of the radical wartime and post-war planning thrust there is no doubt that the public service was expanded dramatically with many more opportunities in local government, education, the health and social care services and elsewhere in the public sector. Quite suddenly being a cricket professional was not so alluring as when it had been something of an escape hatch for talented young men in rather dead-end, boring and often tiring jobs.

For all that there was among the veteran campaigners some sense of enjoyment. Having negotiated the rear end of the 1930s slump and the fortunes of war, it must have been for many a carefree delight to play cricket for weeks on end, even if the train travel was tedious and the guest houses drab. Let two anecdotes suffice to illustrate this point. At an early Cricket Society meeting in London the evening's guest speaker was the long-serving Sussex opening batsman, John Langridge. Asked if he thought playing 34 first-class matches a season was burdensome, he replied warmly that in his day they were sorry when it ended and would have liked to have played more. And at the end of one season Cyril Washbrook's opening partner at Lancashire, the lugubrious Winston Place was asked where he was going for his holidays. 'I've just had mine', he responded laconically.

On the amateur front the story was the reverse. The heavy redistributive taxation concomitant on war and peace ends, both reliant on extensive public finance, meant that upper middle class families could no longer afford the luxury of a cavalier son striding the greensward. Still the counties in the main clung to the convention of the amateur captain, one not always really worth his place cricket-wise and often reliant, were he sensible, on the experienced counsel of his senior professional. The comparative vision of the young, green subaltern and the battle-hardened tough sergeant took time to fade.

An attractive profile from those years which illustrates the point is the lightning career of Ken Cranston, who assuredly did deserve a place in the team. A year or so after demobilisation from the Royal Navy, he played two summers of first-class cricket 1947 and 1948 with eminently virile success as captain of Lancashire and played eight Test matches including the 1947/48 winter tour of the West Indies, captaining England once owing to the indisposition of Gubby Allen. A dental surgeon in the family practice, his father had agreed to subsidise this bright two-year extravaganza. Don Bradman famously sought him out in the England dressing room at Headingley for professional advice Then Ken Cranston had perforce to return to fillings, extractions and very likely stumps for the remainder of his working life. For the post-war amateur it was more likely to be the equivalent of what would now be called a 'gap' year than a settled life-style option.

Ken Cranston, a charming companion, could be gently amusing about post-war county cricket. Once sitting with him at Lord's he spoke of the pastoral nature of some of the out-grounds of less well-resourced counties then. Of one such he remarked that the ground was so green and well-grassed that until the umpires put up the wickets there was no way of telling where the pitch was.

All in all, cricket, as the complimentary phrase then ran, had a good war. The peace seemed momentarily to be fruitful as well. It was not to endure. As the perceptive John Arlott concluded, we were living in 'a kind of cloud cuckoo land'. Thereafter followed something close to implosion during the 1950s, as the following chapter will attempt to describe.

1. Taylor op.cit for background reading on this issue.
2. Ian Kershaw *To Hell and Back; Europe 1914-1949* (2015).
3. F.A.Hayek *The Road to Serfdom* (1944).
4. Jose Harris *William Beveridge; a Biography* (1977).
5. Angus Calder *The People's War; Britain 1939-1945* (1969).
6. Ina Zweiniger-Bargielowska *Austerity in Britain; Rationing, Controls and Consumption* (2000) an award-winning study plentiful in detail and rich in insight in regard of this issue.
7. Midwinter *Collectivist Age* op.cit chapter 18 for a much fuller study of this 1940s theme.
8. Eric Midwinter *The Lost Seasons; Cricket in Wartime 1939-45* (1987) for a more thorough analysis of the often neglected condition of cricket in World War II.
9. John Arlott *Vintage Summer; 1947* (1967) is a predictably first-rate narrative. Eric Midwinter's *Brylcreem Summer; the 1947 Cricket Season* (1991) is a later account of this pivotal time.
10. Sissons op. cit. especially pp.261/272.

Chapter Twelve

Towards Classless Cricket?

In 1951 Tom Dollery became the first modern professional to lead a county championship winning team when Warwickshire were thus victorious. He did so with some trepidation but was decisive enough to refuse his committee's instruction to change in isolation from his team-mates. The officers' mess/headmaster's study mentality of leadership being separated from followers died hard. Several counties chose the same path. Doug Wright at Kent, Dennis Brookes at Northants, Maurice Tremlett at Somerset, Cyril Washbrook at Lancashire and Vic Wilson at Yorkshire were among those appointed during the next ten years.

Elsewhere amateurs continued to rule the roost and travel and accommodation arrangements remained separate, even if different gates had long been banished and dressing rooms were becoming more embracing of both types. The distinction was sustained. Tom Graveney told the anecdote of how he was angrily upbraided by his county captain for calling his friendly England colleague 'David' when the Reverend D.S.Sheppard was playing for Sussex.

It was as if appointing a professional as captain was a last resort, a sign of despair, with counties reverting to amateur captains when a likely (unpaid) lad presented himself; on Cyril Washbrook's retirement the Lancashire committee turned, not altogether satisfactorily, to the amateurs Bob Barber and Joe Blackledge. It was only after a weary spell of English failure that in 1952 Len Hutton was invited to captain England. Stressing that he would not turn amateur, he accepted, although he was succeeded as skipper by the amateur, Peter May. It was not a root and branch change.

In 1953 MCC honoured 26 former England players, all professionals, by making them honorary members of the prestigious club. It was a kindly way of marking their achievements. There may have been a tint of condescension about it, similar to the gold watch retirement ceremony for the trusty, loyal employee but it was far better than simply forgetting or shunning ex-professionals.

Meanwhile, in this last decade of split-class first-class cricket, the amateurs sounded a brave last hurrah. In the 1956 Test at Old Trafford against Australia, ever since titled 'Laker's Match', one interesting fact, alongside the professional off spinner's amazing cull of nineteen wickets, was the English batting line-up. The first five were all amateurs; Peter Richardson, Colin Cowdrey, David Sheppard, Peter May and Trevor Bailey. Shades of the 1900s – and they scored some 350 or so of England's 459 in the first innings of a match recalled more for the poor totals posted by Australia.

Along with Raman Subba Row, Ted Dexter and Bob Barber, English amateur batting ended its long saga on a characteristically flourishing and uplifting note.

For all their efforts, either professional or amateur, the cricketing fabric shrunk in the 1950s and eventually alarm bells faintly began to tinkle if not ring out resoundingly. Where most institutions and activities, economic, social and cultural, had seized or had felt obliged to take the chance offered by the declaration of peace to undertake radical reform, cricket had relaxed complacently, beguiled by what Rowland Bowen called 'the delusion' of the late 1940s.

What was happening nationally was, as ever, the determinant of cricket's destiny. The consensus of a Collectivised society that had reached its zenith in the war and post-war years began to fracture. It was gradual at first, just as the onset of a more co-operative and public-spirited community had taken time to take hold in Victorian Britain. Little more was done to reform society, rather was there a resigned acceptance, with successive governments conserving what was now the new disposition of national assets, grudgingly and unenthusiastically. There was, too, a distinct shift in fiscal and economic methodology. Price and other controls were lifted, subsidies withdrawn and the notion of what had been deliberately something of a siege economy was frowned upon. Much was made of freedom of choice and an end of high taxation, while the pressures of material consumerism, more especially the motor car and television, placed a strain on the old cultural bonds of community life.

For better or for worse, a more pronounced individualism superseded the old-fashioned communitarian values of the previous generations. The 'integrated culture', composed of common denominators in values and activities shared by a strong working class and an earnest middle class, frayed very much at the edges.

Much hinged on the two general elections of 1950 and 1951. It is arguable that, in terms of the future domestic life of British people, they together represent the most meaningful such contests in modern domestic history. One may scarcely overestimate the fundamental nature of the question posed. It was in its best sense an ideological political contest. What the electorate was challenged to decide upon was whether it wished or did not wish for the adoption of a more complete social democracy. The Labour Party campaigned for the former vision of society; the Conservative Party, then true to its implicit principles, sought not to backtrack and destroy but to argue thus far but no further.,

The twin elections were very closely fought. The first gave the Labour Party a thin five seat majority; the second provided the Conservative Party a slightly fatter majority of seventeen. The nation was split into two halves; it could hardly have been closer, with some vague almost unconscious acknowledgement of the primary nature of the decision.

The turnout was 84% in 1950 and 83% in 1951, a tribute to the civic values of the post-war population, the citizenry who had contested the war against totalitarian regimes which would have quailed at the notion of such open, democratic voting. It was tantamount to a 'yes' and 'no' vote, for the total votes for the two main parties in these elections left only 5% and 3% respectively to be shared among the hapless other contenders. Curiously, the Labour Party polled more votes than their opponents in both elections; it was 13.3m against 12.5m in 1950 and 13.9m against 13.7m in 1951, further evidence of the marginal nature of the contests.

There was, then, a genuine shift of mood in the 1950s. There was a loss of confidence in the lofty rationalities that had justified the planning of war and post-war policy. There was a feeling that citizens were too much in the thrall of regiments of unsympathetic clerks of one brand or another. Some of this is intangible. Aneurin Bevan once said that that peoples switch to and fro without reason being dog-like, that is, happily co-operative and companionable, to being cat-like, that is, more haughtily independent and selfish. From hereon in the pendulum swung toward the feline axis. However, the division at this juncture was severe and wide. Analysts of the election results confirmed what observation had intimated – that, at least politically, the non-formal class compact that had endured for close on a hundred years was dissolving.

The crowd became less prominent in the field of leisure. Theatres then cinemas closed by the score. By the end of the century there would only be 500 professional theatres in Britain whereas at the beginning of the century, counting in all the possible theatrical outlets, there were as many as that in the London area alone. Within twenty years of the end of World War II the number of British cinemas had been reduced from 3600 to 1200 with only about one in ten of the population watching a film at least once a month. The great multitudes that had flocked to football matches diminished. Although the mainstream city clubs continued to prosper, smaller clubs which had attracted 30,000 or 40,000 gates in the 1930s and 1940s found themselves playing to sparse gatherings of a few thousands. Football League attendances fell from 44m in the 1949/50 to 28m in the 1964/65 and then 18m in the 1984/85 seasons.

Individualism became the social and cultural as well as the economic and political driver. In terms of the retreat from Collective Leisure, the leading engines of change were television and the motor car. Television, with video players, recording devices and myriad electronic aids in support, magnetised people back towards the home, while, were they to abandon that haven, they became much more likely to do so privately, using the car, and, in consequence of car usage, able to select from a wider range of leisure options.

In 1953 20.5m people, something like half the population, watched the Coronation of Queen Elizabeth II on 5m television sets; within six years there were 15.6m TV sets – and by 1970 well over 90% of household had access to television. The car, initially the non-horse drawn substitute for the rare number of private carriages, became commonplace. Henry Ford's vision of the car as a necessity rather than a luxury came to fruition. The tidal wave of car ownership had reached 4m vehicles in the United

Kingdom by the outbreak of the Second World War. It was seen as the new emblem of the middle classes. By 1970 there were 12m private cars on the roads. In 1959 the first modest stretch of the M1 motorway was declared open, the start of a complex mesh of such highways. It was viewed as a great liberation. During the 1950s and beyond there was a break with the necessarily routine constriction of public transport, with the car releasing the public to seek a much broader gamut of recreation.

Thus were the television set and the motor car the main factors in a return to a much more withdrawn and isolated privy life-style. The home once again, after a hundred years' interlude, became the base for substantial pastimes. Central heating and modern devices helped. The washing machine replaced the public wash-house, the laundry and the laundrette; the TV replaced the cinema. It has been calculated that today's kitchen generates as much power as the average mill in the 1840s. Moreover, as well as witnessing the breakthrough of television, 1953 saw 3m Britons book charter flights for holidays in sunny climes; by 1970 the figure would be 7m, a further fracture in the previous pattern of holiday-making and recreational provision.[1]

Cricket felt the full brunt of this reversion to an 18th century life-style clad in a modern technical garb. There was a double blow. Sir Home Gordon, the well-known cricket commentator of that time, had suggested that it would cost £10,000 a year to organise a county club in the post-war years. The true cost turned out to be nearer £60,000 and by the mid-1950s the counties were already relying on Test revenues for 15% of their income. Attendances shrank alarmingly. 2m, not counting subscribing members, watched the first-class programme in 1950. By the early 1960s this had declined by 75% to 500,000, a massive drop and a descent that showed no signs of abatement.

Cricket, too, was unavoidably involved in the accompanying saga of the dissolution of the British Empire, Having reached its peak in the 1890s, it had all but vanished by the end of the 1960s, making it one of the most short-lived of imperial regimes in history. Benjamin Disraeli's slogan of '*sanitas et imperium*' had tidily summarised the populist concept of an Empire which filled the hearts of the working class with pride and their stomachs with low priced foodstuffs. Disraeli offered the Tory working-class voter the comfort of effective sanitation – his government's 1875 public health act stands proudly as the foundation not just for British physical well-being but for that of many countries - and a focus for enthusiastic loyalty. Politicians such as Joseph Chamberlain and Cecil Rhodes made much of this notion of the Empire as a supplier of both material succour and cultural balm, particularly for the lower classes. Cricket had played a role in this narrative, being accepted, quite accurately, as the *non pareil* imperial sport.

The question of cricket and class in British possessions, in most cases shrouded in a more corrosive cloak of ethnic and racial divisiveness, falls outside the parameters of this study but the ambivalence of English cricket's position imperially does not. Again one senses a strength and a weakness. Curiously enough, it could be argued that of all the British inputs into the erection of their imperial edifice, cricket is by far the most enduring. Almost all former dependencies, whilst abandoning much of the other colonial baggage, still enjoy cricket. Such is its strength; the weakness is that no one else does, at least to top-ranking standards.

The Englishry, the religiosity and the sense of colonial mission that was incorporated into cricket's *diaspora* made it, geopolitically speaking, very lop-sided. Where football, perhaps aided by its later development and conveyed beyond these shores by commercial, engineering and allied agencies, became a global sport, cricket, part of the message carried by the administrator, the teacher, the cleric and the soldier, limited itself to the Empire.

British football gained immensely not just from its global dominance but more directly from its European connections at club as well as national level. Arsenal versus Bayern Munich has never been emulated by Middlesex versus Bavaria. This arose in main part from that upper middle class mind-set, bought into by a willing working class, that cricket was peculiarly English, not even British. At the 1926 Imperial Cricket Conference Lord Harris, the autocratic friend of the professional cricketer, endorsed the edict that a Test match was a fixture 'between sides duly selected by recognised governing bodies representing countries within the Empire.' It was not until 1965, during the phase of the subsidiary changes to cricket in England and elsewhere, that it became, to soothe the ruffled feathers of previously colonised races, the International Cricket Conference. By that time FIFA, established in 1904, had over a hundred members. It now has over 200.

During the late medieval and early modern period when 'play' was uncoordinated and highly localised in Western Europe, it is evident that among the countless species of diversions many which might have gravitated into cricket were enjoyed.[2] There is really no reason why cricket could not have been promoted on the continent in the same way that other British-sourced sporting formats, such as rugby union, tennis and hockey, were – and one writes these heretical words with the feeling of being a blasphemer, such is the intensity of the Englishness of cricket spliced into our cultural bones.

A tome-like anthology could quickly be assembled of rhapsodic prose and verse lauding this xenophobic theme, some of it referenced in literary citations in earlier chapters. In 1833 John Mitford writing in *The Gentleman's Magazine* opined that 'cricket is the pride and privilege of the Englishman alone. Into his noble and favourite amusement no other people ever pretend to penetrate.' Over a hundred years later the message was unchanged. Neville Cardus wrote in 1945 'none except the people of England or of English-speaking countries has excelled at cricket. Its rules and its general legal system tell of the English compromise between individual freedom and corporate responsibility...it somehow holds the mirror up to English nature.'[3]

Every Test-playing nation is a former colonial dependency. One intriguing consequence is that the Cricket World Cup has never been won by a country outside the old imperial boundaries – and not even by England itself, while no nation formerly part of the Empire has ever won the Football World Cup – except, just the once, England, technically a part of the United Kingdom. The International Cricket Conference has ten 'full members', the Test-playing nations, 28 'associate members' and 51 non-voting 'affiliated members', with 29 of the two senior sections hailing from former British possessions. There is scarcely an area of the old British Empire that is not represented on the ICC.

Even before the dissolution of the Empire the keepers of the cricketing flame had had perforce to embrace the obvious fact that members of indigenous races as well as expatriates could become talented cricketers. They had assumed that these 'lesser breeds without the law', as Rudyard Kipling described them, would not be able to cope with so arcane a sport as cricket. In 1900 the *Athletic News* claimed that West Indian 'men of colour' would never 'hope to bring the same amount of intelligence to his game' as the Englishman. But, of course, they could and did.

The cultural answer was to ascribe pseudo-ethnic traits to this phenomenon such as the carefree, joyous West Indian or the magically touched subcontinental. The truth was and is that, slowly, highly talented cricketers took proper advantage of improved facilities, training and structures to reveal themselves as splendid professional – in the vocational sense – players. Ranjitsinhji was an assiduous practiser, not a wizard. Cricketing journalists in particular seemed to relish the idea that a good Indian spin bowler was wily and an English one experienced. Something of cricket's mojo disappeared with the granting of independence to Britain's dependencies. It was no longer the symbol of potent political authority; slowly England and MCC would lose its dominant role as the natural leader and arbiter of post-imperial cricket.

Such economic and cultural buffets were hard to dodge. Top-class cricket, which had never faced up boldly to the question of whether it was part of the entertainment business or part of a kind of moral rearmament project, was in some distress. Reluctantly, the authorities considered reform.

The first move and possibly the simplest from a logistical stance was to acknowledge that the amateur ethic and practice was in decay. As late as 1957/58 a sub-committee chaired by the Duke of Norfolk had asserted that the amateur factor 'was not obsolete, was of great value to the game and should be preserved' but it must have seemed to many a hollow cry. The truth was that the county amateur was a dying species. In the 1930s there were roughly a couple of hundred amateurs in the county championship in a normal season but by the late 1950s this figure was less than forty, with many of these playing but a few games. Nor was there any resolution of the knotty poser of purported amateurs who made a living out of cricket, employed as administrators by their county, writing and broadcasting about the game and even doing a bit of advertising.

It was, then, not altogether surprising that the debate continued and that the Advisory County Cricket Committee late in 1962 determined by the not altogether convincing margin of eleven to seven to abandon the age-old distinction and to label all county players as 'Cricketers.' Thus did the quintessence of class in cricket end with some abruptness. The classic illustration of the cross-alliance was no more.

The 1962 Gentlemen and Players match was the last of a series stretching back to 1806 and comprising 273 games. Although the Players had won double the number in which their opponents were victorious, it is interesting to note that they were by no means in the ascendancy in this last drawn encounter. The Gentlemen scored 323 in their first innings (David Sheppard 112; Ted Dexter 55; Derek Shackleton 4 for 101) and the Players replied with 260 (saved by a couple of late order heroics from Fred Titmus, 70 and Fred Trueman 63, with Trevor Bailey taking 6 for 58). The Gentlemen declared on 172 for 5 (Roger Prideaux 109) but the Players comfortably engineered the draw with 207 for 3 (John Edrich 77 not out, and Peter Parfitt 63).

Before further examining the social significance of this decision it might be worthwhile listing the other reforms introduced at the same time or just after this eminent pronouncement. The merit in this lies in the sudden feeling in the cricket world that modernisation must be effected. The termination of the old-fashioned device of Gentlemen and Players was a preface to some minor structural reform, an intrepid dipping of the cautious toe into the waters of change.

There were three major interlocking elements. In ten years beginning in 1963, three one-day tournaments were introduced which, compared with the calm of the previous fifty years, was restlessness indeed. The Gillette Cup, at first 65 overs, later 60 overs, was launched with £6500 funding, after a very close vote on the Advisory County Cricket Committee. It was followed by the John Player Sunday League of 40 overs in 1969 and the Benson and Hedges Cup, a combine of mini-leagues and knock-out play, in 1972. There was, as is well known, considerable massaging of the rules to encourage attractive batting with restriction on bowlers and field-placements.

Next, it was decided in 1968 to permit counties to employ overseas players. Eligibility rules had been relaxed in general since World War II and the switch of players from one county to another had become more frequent but this direct boost to non-English recruitment brought many star players into the game over the next decades. Thirdly, and as the signing of the limited-overs competitions bear testimony, there was sponsorship. In place of the old-time dependence on wealthy patrons, English cricket pinched its nose and turned to the commercial sector and raised funds in return for advertising branding.

The limited overs competitions certainly helped to bring back the crowds in some degree but whether they were in sufficient numbers to underwrite the high salaries of overseas celebrities is doubtful. The three novel devices formed a spiral of employing international stars to play one-day cricket funded by sponsors so that international stars could be employed to play one-day cricket funded by sponsors.

At another serious level, the introduction of the limited overs tournaments was justified as a conduit for attracting people to watch the first-class game. From this stance it was a flop. With seven-a-side rugby the shorter format is used as an appetiser or fillip fore and aft of the season; there has never been any peril of it supplanting the mainstream game. With cricket's shortened version, the reverse is largely true. The limited overs variety flourished as the county championship, as a spectator sport, continued to diminish. The one-day tail wagged the three or four-day dog. There followed the advent of costumes that made cricketers look like plumbers or car mechanics. The was much agitation among the faithful, who found little solace in the knowledge that white had only become ubiquitously fashionable during the Victorian era of cricket's association with goodness, *circa* 1880 to 1895. Before that there had been coloured clothing. For instance, the All-England XI had worn white shirts with pink spots. They might have been mistaken for Tottenham Hotspur or Derby County in their away strip.

The limited overs game increasingly made itself manifest as somehow separate from the first-class formula rather than its adjunct and feeder. John Arlott had perhaps been wise in his days when he advised that the one-day variety was fine in itself but it should be given another name and not be called cricket. George Bernard Shaw had, from his acerbic Dubliner stance, once written that 'the English are not very spiritual people so they invented cricket to give them some sense of eternity'. As the 20th century wore on the English public had apparently grown agnostic in this regard.

To look ahead a reasonable time, over the next twenty ot thirty years after these changes, by the early 1990s the first-class annual attendances had shrunk by almost a half again to 170,000. That opened up an ever-widening gulf since the 2m of 1950 and the close on 3m of 1947. To underline the seriousness of the decline, in 1990 some counties were counting themselves lucky if, over the season, as many as 10,000 customers paid at the turnstiles for their first-class programme. In 1947 12,000 paid to watch the first day of the varsity match. The notion that the shorter would usher the public into watching the longer version of the game was dead in the water.

The county finances were little better, even if changed in composition. In the 1990s, only 8% of county revenue derived from paying customers and 17% from membership subscriptions. The remaining 75% was gleaned from commercial and TCCB sources. To detail the alteration in terms of one county, in 1962, at the launch of this raft of reforms, Lancashire's turnover was £67.000, £39,000 of which was taken at the turnstiles or in subscriptions. The rest came chiefly from internal commercial enterprise, with only £8000 in Test and broadcasting receipts. In 1990 the turnover had shot up to £2m but only £0.5m was in gate-money and subscription, a proportionate drop from 60% to 25%%, while £1.5m came mainly from

Test and one-day international receipts, plus substantive local ventures into club sponsorship, all-year-round catering and advertising.

Two other changes must be recorded, one little and parochial, the other large and global. In 1967 the (Professional) Cricketers' Association was established with Fred Rumsey of Somerset and Jack Bannister of Warwickshire the early key leaders. Within a few years most county cricketers had become members and among one or two other gains, it persuaded the counties to agree to a minimum wage and found itself sitting on relevant national committees.[4]

The paternalism of the upper and middle class MCC and county authorities and the deference, even, one might add, the fear of victimisation, of the working class employees had delayed such an enterprise for generations. It was a further aspect of the perception of cricket as somehow rarefied, not to be tainted by ordinary criteria. Even in 1967 some on both sides of the divide were shocked by the concept. One has noted that this same anxiety about any sort of unionism was evident in some charities where the lofty tone of the rationale rendered anything so contentious as staff negotiation sordid. It was like having a trade union for vicars.

Fears of likely militancy were soon proved bootless. TCCB funding, initially £20,000 annually, queered the partisan pitch immediately. Imagine the National Coal Board coughing up for Arthur Scargill's salary in the 1980s. That entwining of interests apart, the whole venture had more the character of a staff association or a professional body and not that of a trade union that might contemplate affiliating to the Trade Union Congress. That is not a criticism of the PCA which has achieved several beneficial results for its members. This is an observation about its nature. It was more the British Dental Association than the Boiler-makers Union – and that was of a piece with the prevailing middle class nature of its members which will the chief theme of the following chapter.

This was a tremor compared with the earthquake triggered by Kerry Packer in 1977.[5] Apart from raising the tempo, financing and design, inclusive of the use of coloured clothing, of limited overs international cricket, the well-known Packer saga scratched at a sore on the body of cricket that no one had hitherto thought or dared to tamper with. Mr Justice Slade in the High Court declared that the ICC and TCCB ban on Packer-contracted players was unreasonable restraint of trade. What for the best part of a hundred years had been common employment practice was illegal. What had been fairly obvious but never before subjected to a legal challenge was shown to be wrong.

The ramifications were enormous. In a phrase, English cricketers, national and county, were from now on in employment rather than in service, with carefully constructed contracts not feudalistic obligations. Even recently counties have found it necessary to offer players a year-round contract and salary because of moves to poach their staffs for overseas winter cricketing outside their control.

It was akin to the freeing of the football labour force. In 1960/61 the maximum wage decree was overruled and in 1964 the George Eastham case against Newcastle United, also heard in the High Court, demonstrated that the Football League registration system was an unfair restraint of trade. Footballers were accorded the rights that appertained to all workers. The scene was set for the forthcoming explosion of wages and movement in the theatre of football. The difference was that the Professional Footballers Association had been chiefly instrumental in, with the occasional threat of strike action, procuring their ends, while cricketers had had to await the boldness of a maverick capitalist, the one with the most riches, to find their legal rights assured and protected.

Football is simple; cricket is complex, be it as games or in structures. The Corinthian virtues of football, with ex-public schoolboy teams winning the first dozen or so FA Cups, a competition based on the Harrow Cock House trophy, were lost in the thickening mists of passing time. Professional football had soon become a straightforward business of bosses and workers, except that, compared with most enterprises, the workers eventually emerged with exceptional rewards. Cricket, with its more complicated web of relationships of paternalistic governors and usually complicit servants, sharing a belief in the sport's special ethos, struggled to find its bearings in a world entirely dedicated to marketing and monetary yardsticks. On the model of the likes of Herbert Sutcliffe and Wally Hammond, the professional players sought to emulate the amateur gentlemen, believing this to be their chosen mode of travel.

Let us observe, next, to what extent they succeeded.

---

1. Midwinter *Collectivism* op cit; the final section of this text analyses this switch to a more Individualistic epoch in considerable detail.
2. John Eddowes *The Language of Cricket* (1997) provides a fascinating *entree* to this subject.
3. Neville Cardus *English Cricket* (1945).
4. Sissons op. cit. especially pp 285-292 .
6. Wynne-Thomas op. cit. pp 229-236 for a most concise summation of the Packer reformation.

Chapter Thirteen
Change of Culture; Change of Cricket

A respectable working-class family and a rather serious-looking middle-class family strolled through the municipal park where two or three cricket matches were ongoing. Both families paused for a few minutes to listen to the district brass band in the bandstand playing a programme of 'Gems from *The Gondoliers*'. Then they walked to the bus stop by the park gate. They caught the corporation bus and took the short trip to their local Odeon cinema to watch Celia Johnson and Trevor Howard starring in *Brief Encounter*.

That little cameo of life in the late 1940s is salutary in that the half a dozen or so specific items listed there have either vanished or become outmoded. The civic and co-operative pattern of community existence and the communal sensibility associated with it were undermined by the onrush of neo-liberalism. The Tolkien-like term 'middle England' was coined much later but it might well have been utilised for that earlier period, given its middling characterisation. With the central phalanx of Britons acting and believing in cross-class unison, everything gravitated towards the mean. For instance, although newspapers varied from the *Daily Telegraph* to the *News of the World*, they were all recognisable as coming from the same stable, compared with the chasm today, say, between the *Times* and the *Sun*. A literary phenomenon of the age was emblematic; in 1935 Allen Lane founded Penguin books. At 6d a copy, he demonstrated the ready market for serious reading; Woolworths stores bought 63,000 books immediately and in the first ten months alone 1m books were printed.

The middlebrow was dominant then. In late Victorian and Edwardian England few paused to ponder whether a Dickens novel was popular or classic or whether W.P.Firth's paintings of *The Derby Day* or *The Railway Station* should be similarly categorised. The cultural gaps did tend to open a little before the 1950s, with atonal music, abstract art and free association literature being examples but they widened much further as the century wore on.

Other factors contributed to the collapse of the old integrated culture.[1] First there was a generational element, especially as 'youth' came, by common observation and by its own self-awareness, to be a separatist bloc, with its own sounds, costume, argot and other accoutrements. Second, and more tellingly, there was the sheer diversity of communication, with, for example, a welter of television channels and other outlets. Such a wealth of choice had its welcome and beneficial aspect but it spelled the end of a collective enjoyment and appreciation. The cultural niches were highly individualised. Moreover, the entirety of cultural experience increased in tempo, creating a nervy whirligig of fast-moving, ephemeral, ever-changing activity. 'Freedom to choose what is always the same' is the verdict of one commentary.[2]

It should be added in parenthesis, given the rather gloomy tone of these prognostications, that there were many faults in the older regime of the integrated culture. It could be and often was narrow-minded, censorious, discriminatory, puritanical, oppressive and much else besides. The point at issue is that it was 'congregational' in foundation and that it was replaced by a social structure that was more self-based.

This 'desegregated culture' was, of course, an echo of an economic and political tone in which self and money were the reigning arbiters. For good or ill, and particularly after the oil price crisis of the early 1970s, there was a wholesale abandonment of regulatory processes for the banking and financial markets, the privatisation in whole or part of public utilities, a reduction in state expenditure, especially directed at the welfare budget, and a major lowering of taxation.

This more libertarian approach, in terms of social class, created a much more unequal society materially as well as socially and culturally. Both major political parties and their leaders, be it Margaret Thatcher or Tony Blair, naturally sought to robe the fundamental shifts in the guise of modernisation but, in reality, it amounted to a basic reversal to the free-for-all decades of the 18th and early 19th centuries. For example, the zero hours contracts and the enforced spread of under-paid self-employment re-invented the severe casualisation of labour of that earlier period while the system of subsidising employers and landlords via tax credits and housing benefits was distinctly reminiscent of the old poor law before its strict restructuring in 1834.

The gradual moves in the later decades of the 19th and the opening decades of the 20th centuries towards a more egalitarian society were drastically reversed. The United Kingdom is now the fourth most unequal of the OECD's 34 nations. The top fifth take 60% of the available income and the bottom fifth 0.6%. To be in the top one per cent now requires a couple with no children to be earning £160,000 a year. In 2015 Oxfam suggested that the five richest families in the UK had as much wealth as that of the 20% of the population that comprised its poorest section.

The Poverty and Social Exclusion Group produced in 2014 *Poverty Now*, billed as 'the most detailed study of poverty in Britain.' It showed that the number of households living at or below minimum living standards, defined as being without three or more of the basic necessities of life, had risen from 14% to 33%. The number living in temporary accommodation in 2015 was 49,000 families, a rise of 25% in five years, and inclusive of 93,000 children. Early in 2015 the Joseph Rowntree Trust published findings that showed that four in ten of British families with children, in all 8m people, were on incomes below the minimum required to participate adequately in society. 22% of the actual work-force earned less than the 'living wage' and many districts had food-banks. As in Hanoverian days, the under-class received punishment, not socialisation.

These changes have produced what some sociologists are calling an 'hourglass society', although, in truth, the British version does not have the symmetry of its twin globes. Nonetheless, a form of social exclusion at both top and bottom of society has evolved, with both a large sub-class and a very wealthy elite engaged in extremely different life-styles. The late Victorian/early 20th century 'middle way', where there was the reality and the self-perception of common ground among what amounted to the bulk of the population has vanished. And it was during that period that first-class cricket enjoyed its finest hours.

The concomitant of a low-tax society - the decline of public expenditure and services – was tangible. Alongside this was a wholesale demolition of local government, the potency of which had been so remarkable a factor in the Victorian and later eras. A much more centralised regime evolved. The proportion of British public spending controlled by the central state as against that of local government is 72%; it is 35% in France and 17% in Germany. In the late 1890s the central contribution in the UK was only 14%. The historian Jose Harris claims that the United Kingdom has moved 'from one of the most localised and voluntaristic countries in Europe to one of the most centralised and bureaucratic'.[3]

Both impoverished public services and stricken municipal administration are well illustrated by the fate of a communal and municipal amenity which had earlier served cricket admirably: the park. In 2014 86% of parks departments reported cuts of up to 50%, parts of the £42m reduction in local sports and leisure budgets over the 2010-2015 parliament. It is a short-sighted view castigated by the Sport and Recreation Alliance as 'storing up problems for the longer term.' Local authority sport and recreation spending was cut from £1.4bn in 2009/10 to £1bn in 2013/14 and prices increased dramatically leading to a sharp decline in sporting participation.

The main comparison to be drawn between the pre-1850 and the post-1950 epochs must be the high rate of lawlessness. After a long era of abnormally low crime figures, criminal activity grew alarmingly. It jumped from under 0.5m yearly criminal offences in the 1940s to 15m reported and unreported offences in the 1990s. There has been some slight decrease since but crime remains very high by earlier standards. There were 21 woundings formally recorded in 1921; there were over 100,000 in 2002. The relevant demographic ratios show there were in the 1940s 250 estimated annual crimes per 100,000 of the population compared with 11,000 per 100,000 in the 1990s. Whatever variables there may be in these figures, the astronomical scale of the figures removes all doubt about the extent of the crime wave. In 1939 200,000 crimes were reported to the police; in 2004 it was 5.7m.

The term 'nonconformist conscience' is often used to define the mind-set of the population in the hundred or so years before 1950. It is difficult to avoid the judgement that this ethical focus on social behaviour has been largely abandoned. Jeffrey Richards' simple formula of the 'rough' and the 'respectable' in constant duelling is a useful tool in this regard. As he himself has argued, the 'rough' element is once again enjoying the ascendant, as it did in Hanoverian times.[4]

Crime and occasional rioting was not the only source of misconduct. What criminologists call 'incivilities' became rife, with vandalism, graffiti, noise and raucous behaviour commonplace. Of particular note from a sporting standpoint was the consistent week-in-week-out violence of football crowds which peaked in the 1980s but is still a matter of concern. The introduction of all-seater stadia and attempts to rein in the consumption of alcohol have helped but the fact that careful segregation of fans, unheard of in earlier years, with heavy policing and stewarding, demonstrates that the problem is being coped with, even taken for granted, rather than solved. Commentators criticise clubs and the police when supporters are enabled to clash almost as if such violent behaviour was normal conduct unless tamed.

An exhaustive broadsheet critique of the current situation ended with the pertinent reminder that 'all the preceding points would be rendered null and void if grown men could attend a football match and not do such things as tear a seat out from its bracket and hurl it at another person. It is remarkable how so little of the discussion is given over to the basic requirement for adults to behave in a socially acceptable manner'[5]

It is fair to say that if the public order legislation relating to likely disorder at political parades or meetings was applicable to football, hundreds of fixtures would be cancelled, such is the nuisance caused not so much inside but around the grounds. In a phrase, the crowd came to be feared again – as it had been in Hanoverian times. It is instructive to recall how well-conducted society was when the Football League was formed all those years ago in 1888 when the authorities had rightly grown comfortable about large gatherings.

It was perhaps fortunate that football crowds had diminished and the major disorder was around the big city clubs; had the gates remained as large as in the 1930s and 1940s the weekly unrest would have been difficult to police. Cricket was possibly lucky in that, apart from some days of some Test matches and high-level one day games, there were no crowds large enough to cause trouble. It is also true that the tighter time intensity of football makes for a higher octane atmosphere than cricket and the football tribal rivalries are more ferocious. Action has sometimes been taken to restrain alcohol abuse but there have been no reports of coachloads of young Gloucestershire supporters alighting at Taunton tooled up for combat with their Somerset counterparts. One might speculate that where alcohol is suspected to fuel football hooliganism, it acts as a further sleep inducement for cricket fans.

Gradually another factor came into play, one that is of much significance for the story of class relationship to sport. A further response, at least in the upper tiers of football where the crowds remained sizable and the troubles threatened, was a mighty heft in the ticket prices. Obviously the major motive for this policy was a financial one but it had the attendant social effect of aiding in the restoration of comparative order. It is true, of course, that not all football hooligans were or are working class youths; the court records show that some older men in middle class occupations were among the guilty parties. However, Premiership prices nowadays are outside the range of those other than with high and, importantly, for spectating is a regular habit, stable incomes.

By the 2007/08 football season the proportion of Premier League spectators from social categories C2, D and E, the definitive working class element, was down to 25%. This was a complete reversal from the 1940s and before when the working class percentage had been an estimated 75% or 80%.[6]

From the 1880s to 1946 it cost 1s for an adult to watch a Football League game; from 1946 it was 1s3d; 1950, 1s9d and by 1960 2s or 2s6d. Since then, and with the massive increase of wage bills, it has ballooned. It has been calculated that the minimum salary required to afford regular Premiership spectating is £38,000, against a national average income of £26,000. This effectively precludes four-fifths of the population from watching mainstream football, with younger people perhaps especially affected. The average age of an adult Premier League season ticket holder is 41.[7]

That scenario is easily transferable to cricket, even if the social research may not be as rigorous or as available as that for football. For major international and other prestigious matches the prices have risen substantially. In cricket's golden age it was possible to enjoy a day at the Australian Test at Lord's for a shilling. For peak days now it could be a £100 or £110. The comparison of ratios is startling. It is an increase of 2000 times. As a fraction of the relative weekly earnings, it is a rise from 1% to 20%. One ticket would cost one-fifth of the weekly income for the average household, realistically ruling out the vast majority. The Lord's Test possibly presents the extreme case but pricing everywhere is comparatively high by former standards. County memberships remain at reasonably high levels but, as hitherto, are very much the province of older loyalists and die-hards with steady incomes. The small coteries of a few thousand who have stayed to worship the beautiful game at county level are resolutely middle-class. The alternative myth – that working class people did not watch first-class cricket – has finally been proved genuine where once it was not. The gentrification of cricket moves on apace.

During a seven year period when I had the enjoyable task of editing the MCC annual or yearbook I attended an interesting meeting about advertising revenue, the hope being that with a circulation of well over 20,000 that might easily be found. The advertising consultant soon dispelled that aspiration, indicating that the demographic was exceedingly narrow, as in male (as was then the case) almost entirely A and B in social category and average age 71. 'Why would a manufacturer of bras for young women be attracted?', he asked rhetorically. There was a whispered riposte about a possible niche audience and then we moved on to next business.

The County Championship continues to be the loser. The actual figures for spectators at all domestic and international cricket is not so appalling. Between 1997 and 2015 the annual attendances were roughly 1.5m to 2.3m, the wideness of the range a reflection of weather and the popularity of the tourists. The total of subscribing members to the county clubs, including the high MCC figure, is around 150,000. The advent of Twenty20 cricket has also been a valued shot in the arm - but the numbers attending first-class county matches are in pitiful decline.

In the 2015 season Warwickshire did well in welcoming 37.000 paying customers to its eight home matches but other counties did badly. Glamorgan, Leicestershire and Derbyshire managed only 11,000 or 12,000 while Northants found little more than 4000 hopefuls coming to its doors. Overall there were some 300,000 paying attendees at county matches in 2015. The average daily attendance, exclusive of members, was thus a maximum of just over a thousand and a minimum of 120.[8]

The decline of support for first-class county cricket did not, happily for the players, deter the increase in cricketers' salaries over this latter period. The Packer episode had blown apart the previous contractual device and, in all branches of the entertainment industry, there were quite radical improvements in pay.

The revolution was more dramatic in football than in cricket. Wally Hammond's cautious choice of cricket as the better financial deal would have been patently the wrong one from the late 20th century onwards. There was an intriguing counterpoint in the sporting headlines of *the Manchester Evening News* about the turn of the century announcing that Andrew Flintoff was requesting £50,000 for the season at one Old Trafford and Roy Keane £50,000 a week at the other – the latter was more successful (£52,000) than the former (£32,000) in his negotiations. In another example from the same two bastions was the destiny of Phil Neville. On leaving school he was offered something in the region of £1800 for the summer at the cricketing Old Trafford and £1500 a week at the footballing one. It should be added that, as a fifteen year old, he was assessed by a high-ranking Lancashire official, one not given to melodramatic utterances, as being the best schoolboy batsman he had ever seen. The Manchester United manager Alex Ferguson, recalling the incident when the young tyro asked which sport he should select, said he thought Phil Neville was taking the piss.

Had, as now, football been an all-year-round sport in mid-20th century, it is certain that the likes of Wally Hammond or Denis Compton would never have been seen on a cricket field. Figures across the sporting board from Barclay's bank in 2006 revealed that county cricketers were earning an average of £43,000 annually, with something of a gap between Surrey's £51,000 to £60,000 and Glamorgan's £31,000. Self-evidently, contracted England players made considerably more money. Premiership footballers were on average earning £665,000 a year or £884,000 if sponsorships were included. In 2015 Wayne Rooney's wealth was said to be £72m, placing him among the world's richest sportsmen. The England football captain in the 1930s, Arsenal's Eddie Hapgood, never made more than £250 a year – and when in later life he fell on hard times, Arsenal sent him £30. Even the players in the lowly League Two, the old Fourth Division, were in yearly receipt of £49,000 in 2006 while among other team games senior British Rugby Union club players had salaries averaging £60,000.

Even if the top footballers are now earning five times as much as the top cricketers, the latter are still well rewarded at something like twice the average national income, with the star international players earning tidy sums. There is then a curious twist in the basic context of this study. By the usual yardsticks of income, education, housing and allied adjuncts, there is no doubt that all professional cricketers are now middle class.

First-class cricket is now a single class occupation where once it was a cross-class activity. What happened when the division of Players and Gentlemen was abandoned and all those involved became simply 'Cricketers' was that they all soon correspondingly became 'Gentlemen', at least in social class terms. The aspirations of Herbert Sutcliffe, Wally Hammond and their ilk finally came to perfect fruition.

Given the previous argument that the vast majority of county members and paying spectators are middle-class, as assessed by income, the first-class game in England is by and large a middle-class entertainment for a middle-class clientele.

The fact that many England players have been educated at fee-paying schools serves to underpin that claim, even allowing for James Anderson's schooling at St Theodore's Roman Catholic High School, Burnley. 73% of the England team that won the Ashes in 2015 were educated at fee-paying schools.[9] The story of state schools and cricket has been a patchy one with some regions more active than others in this respect over the years. There was quite a lot of cricket played during the relatively brief recrudescence of grammar schools, from about the 1920s to the 1960s, for they were often eager to mimic the habits of the fee-paying schools. However, the many secondary schools in heavily urbanised areas always suffered from inadequacy of grounds, a plight deepened in the later years of the 20th century by many sales of sports fields for building development. As an example of the differences, it was reported in 2009 that Dulwich College, a fee-paying establishment of 1450 boys in the London Borough of Southwark where the annual fees then were £27,330 well above the then average national earnings, had eight cricket pitches. The borough's fourteen secondary schools, serving a population of nearly 300,000, had only six such amenities among them. A full boarder's fee at Dulwich is now £39,480.

The continuing cricketing dominance of the fee-paying sector reflected their old-fashioned belief that cricket was some kind of *alfresco* scripture lesson. A major factor has been the furtherment of an alternative educative opinion. Comprehensive education involves a comprehensive view about physical, health and leisure education, a concept that attempts to provide a wide range of 'taster' sports in the hope that individual pupils will find one or more that appeals to them and aids both their bodily health and general enjoyment. Cricket is not ignored, neither is it sanctified. Indeed, and although junior forms of the game such as kwik cricket have been devised, cricket is not the most effective pastime, educationally speaking. At any one time nine out of 22 participants are sedentary with others only marginally involved. The actual game as a physical exercise is thus limited in effectiveness.

Cricket cannot lay a claim, educationally, to any more priority than any other sport. It is no longer, if it ever were, the 'national sport'. The notion that a school should concentrate on the cultivation of its first eleven in order that the cricketing section of the entertainment industry should be resourced is a palpable nonsense.

As for recreational cricket, that is probably in a healthier state than it has ever been, precisely because the sport itself has taken more responsibility for its roots and flowerings and not abandoned the task to schools which have a much more profound purpose. Especially since 1997 with the introduction of a pyramidal shape for English cricket through the county cricket boards and the wholesale acceptance of league competitions, this has been a wholesome development. Lancashire, to take one instance, has 22 leagues comprising 276 clubs, all running two or three sides and, very importantly, energetically offering cricket at youth and junior levels, beginning with under nines. The county boards manage regional teams beginning as young as thirteen, so that opportunities do exist on a major scale, certainly more so than at any time in cricket's history.

This is something about which to feel pleased. Those of us who enjoyed compulsory school cricket will, if our consciences and memories are clear, recall the misery of those who didn't. Apart from a few whose fathers force them to attend out of deluded hopes of future reflected glory, the children going along to club coaching sessions are volunteers. The only note of anxiety to express is that cricket, with all its paraphernalia of kit and equipment, is an expensive game. That must be a deterrent to many and subscribe to the concept of a cricket as a middle class province.

Most of that is wholesome enough. Cricket takes its place among a score of other possible sporting pastimes without being, either in support or prestige, any better or worse than the others. An ECB survey in September 2016 worried cricket's powers-that-be more than a trifle when it reported that fewer than a third of children recognised a picture of Alastair Cook, with a greater number identifying all-in wrestlers. So be it. The halcyon era when cricket prided itself on preeminence in the sporting hierarchy had passed.

Thus while the recreational game and the limited overs variations continue in relatively good health, what makes for anxiety is first-class cricket at sub-international level. Since the inception of a formalised country-wide stratum of cricket during the 19th century, the county system had been its keystone, enabling it to substantiate the explicit claim for cricket to be regarded and respected as the national sport *par excellence.*

A combine of the Packer explosion that demolished the cosy low pay mode with the abrupt and seemingly unstoppable decline in customer support has left first-class county cricket in destitute shape. High salaries and low attendances make for an uneconomic catastrophe.

The counties are in hock to the national ruling body the ECB, all of them being reliant on annual grants therefrom, much of this funding the fruits of televised cricket. This power requires them to release talented players to accept England contracts which curtail their appearances for the counties to the detriment of the pleasures of county watchers. Unlike the old days – 'Len Hutton, Yorkshire and England' – casual fans are often unable to identify from which county some England players have emanated. It has reached a pretty pass where top players have played more first-class matches for England than for their counties. That, of course, is in part a consequence of playing many more international fixtures than hitherto but it is scant compensation for the loyal county member deprived of a sighting of his or her county's best players.

To test that dominion of national over club cricket, visualise the wrath of such football managers as Arsene Wenger or Pep Guardiola were their star players removed from their squads for continuous international duty.

However, that central domination is not total. The England cricket authorities do need a readily well-filled sump from which to draw players suited for international performance. It makes for an uneven and uneasy relationship. The county circuit is not as fit for purpose as it should be but any attempt to uproot it and create a fresh base is and would be met by strenuous disapproval. The county turkeys would refuse to vote for an ECB Christmas. The ECB control is immensely strong, as Durham's 2016 punitive treatment – relegation to the second division and a 48 point penalty in exchange for a £3.8m bail-out – for financial failings bears witness. Nevertheless, any talk of mergers or closures of county clubs find all the county clubs clinging together in 'I am Spartacus' mood.

In its modern role as a conveyor belt for TV funded international first-class and one-day teams, the current county system fails on two serious counts. As to size, it is certainly too cumbersome for its function as a womb for England cricketers. Australia might benefit from a slightly wider range of first-class cricket below Test level but seems to trundle along steadily enough with only about 50 top-class professional players. Conversely, it could be argued that the English county pattern is too sparse in incidence to offer regular top-class cricket to all parts of the UK.

Eighteen teams playing sixteen games frequently in almost empty grounds; 'Much Bowling in the Morgue'; this was a descriptor I utilised many years ago when many would have more readily picked up the Richard Murdoch / Kenneth Horne reference. It related personally and specifically to watching a county game at Trent Bridge on a fine summer's morning. For an hour or so there was a glittering duel, a feast of cricketing artistry, between Richard Hadlee and David Gower. It was chastening to note that there was but a few score of spectators scattered about that splendid and well-appointed arena.

If international cricket is to be the sole criterion, then four or five bases, as to both player production and venues, would be sufficient, as appears to be the case in other Test-playing countries. But if the yardstick were about offering high-class cricket as a nationwide entertainment, eighteen stadia would not be sufficient nor would all the existing ones be at the most propitious points. The Football League offers a reasonable standard of professional football in 92 locations, not forgetting 42 teams in the Scottish leagues and twelve in the Northern Irish premiership. One does not have to travel far to watch a fortnightly game.

The interconnectedness of these national divisions emphasises the second flaw in the county structure. It is very rigidified. As of the 2016/2017 season 47 different teams have competed in the twenty-strong English Premier League in just 25 seasons. In the National League, the one just below the three divisions of the Football League, there are no less than thirteen teams that have hitherto played in the superior layers – and there are four or five more in the two feeder competitions to the National League. That is football's testament to the rise and fall of sporting mobility.

Now consider the sheer inflexibility of county cricket. In the last hundred years two counties – Glamorgan and Durham – have joined the county fray and none have departed. There were mild post-WWII flirtations with Devon and Buckinghamshire but they came to nothing. The impulsion to strive and change is absent. Elsewhere I have compared the county championship with two Forts; Knox for getting in and Colditz for getting out.

The other factor in this restrictiveness is the compulsory shire styling. Previous mention was made in these pages of the extraordinary narrowness of the origins of first-class cricket clubs, the two major universities with their strong links with the counties being the only other additions of enduring note to the first-class roster. Currently, it is unlikely that any of the twenty Minor County Clubs would consider the financial perils of first-class status, rather preferring the homely comforts of a three day competition of almost entirely amateur standing. English cricket has never searched for a broader range of first-class pedigree club births.

Some readers may feel the constant comparisons with association football may have some degree of unfairness about them. It will be urged that the games are totally different in character. But that is part of the issue. The two games had a common origin as national sports in their formalisation by ex-public schoolboys and until about 1900 enjoyed parity of both esteem and popular support. Indeed, cricket probably had the edge before the Edwardian era. Other sports are less visible or less nationwide. Rugby Union took a slightly different route both socially and geographically while Rugby League kept for the most part to a strictly regional core. Of other field team sports, hockey and lacrosse never made significant steps towards crowd-pleasing enterprise. Many sports fans boast of a joint allegiance to a cricketing county and a football team. It does make room for some reasonable comparability.

Whatever the case, association football in England, aggressively commercial and resolved to maintain the ethos of being an element in the entertainment industry, has swept ahead of cricket as the national sport in both the popular and the cultural sense. First-class county cricket in particular has taken a back seat.

What role did class play in what might critically be described as this undermining of English first-class cricket?

1. Midwinter *the Collectivist Age* op.cit.
2. T.W.Adorno & M.Harkheimer *Dialectic of Enlightenment* (1997) p.166/7.
3. J.Harris *Civil Society in British History* (2004).
4. Richards op. cit.
5. *Guardian* 28 Oct 2016.
6. Adrian Tempany *And the Sun Shines Now* (2016).
7. M.Johnes & M.T.Taylor *Football Ticket prices; Some Lessons from History* in *History and Policy* Feb 2016.
8. *Wisden 2016.*
9. Anthony Clavane *A Yorkshire Tragedy;the Rise and Fall of a Sporting Powerhouse* (2016) This book examines how Yorkshire's sporting glory, rooted in its heavy industrial culture, became irrevocably dimmed in the neo-liberal era.

Chapter Fourteen
First-Class Fragility

People may or may not get the governments they deserve but they certainly get the cultural baggage and social paraphernalia they deserve. The economic and political construct of any society determines in major part its style of leisure, arts, pastimes and allied domestic values and habits. That is baldly true in that, for example, a national format of any game is impossible without an effective transport system and other means of communication. But it is also true in the more nuanced manner in which the social practice and conventional beliefs of a community intertwine with and influence the character of its cultural superstructure.

It is equally true that in the fluidly organic movement of community or national life, there are overlaps and vestiges. It is at least arguable that cricket in its Victorian guise as a three or four day county-orientated diversion might be so identified. To recap briefly, the county system that evolved or was devised during the last third of the 19th century was, by accident or design or more likely a compound of both, an adjunct to the cross-class alliance that was the prevailing *Zeitgeist*.

Its leading features were a resolve to find, despite its cumbersome qualities, an accommodation by which paid working class and notionally unpaid middle class players could perform in tandem and by which both classes were offered a satisfactory chance of spectating. Uppermost in this determination were shared values, especially relating to a genuinely felt if actually false pastoral imagery, a proud and superior sense of imperial splendour and a firm belief in the Victorian gloss on Christian morality. Ineluctably, these three aspects were closely interlinked; for instance Rudyard Kipling's 'White Man's Burden' was accepted as a Christian obligation.

Crucially, nationwide cricket, in both its professional and recreational formats, was encouraged by industrialism, especially by way of vastly improved transport and other means of communication. Victorian cricket was in part a creature of the Industrial Revolution, the provincial manufacturing cities becoming sites for the game's national spread at its highest level. Indeed, a further perspective on the current increasing centralisation of government is the return of the nation to one dominated by the south-eastern conclave. In the pre-industrial era of the 18th century and before, London was basically the only major power-house, with trade and population intensely based on the area south of a line from Bristol to Norwich. It was the great industrialised towns of, in particular, the north and the midlands, cities like Leeds, Birmingham and Manchester, that had exerted the keenest edge of local government hegemony, just as they had provided bases for national and international cricket. The decline of the provincial manufacturing base and the renewal of the sheer monetary agency of London and its surrounds is at one with that retrogression to a centralised state, almost wholly lacking the checks and balances of strong municipal involvement.

Most critical of all, for close on a hundred years there was the relative calm of public demeanour, with a low crime rate, a high level of community discipline and deference and a strong sentiment of acceptable social behaviour. It has been acknowledged in this text that this had its downside of Puritanical censoriousness but, by and large, the crowd could be trusted.

It is remarkable how neatly cricket fitted into this social and cultural frame of reference. So tidy is the fit that it is possible to view cricket as a microcosm of society in those decades. It was distinctly middle brow, taking its place, in terms of leisure, alongside the Gilbert and Sullivan operas, the novels of Charles Dickens, the cinema and BBC radio in their shared golden epoch, the public library and the municipal park and one or two other bygone cultural icons. These former staples also had a solidity and a more subdued quality, even a slower tempo, than much of modern pastimes which, however enjoyable and brilliant, often generate an ephemeral, racier, fast-moving pace.

The difficulty arose when the referential frame was excessively re-carpentered. Interestingly, the new frame looks very much like the pre-1830s frame, as has been previously hinted. Just to take a tiny cricketing example, the gambling, corruption and misbehaviour that disfigured the game in the Hanoverian and Regency eras has returned. There are moves to give umpires 'red card' dismissal powers, such is the disruptive attitude of some players, especially in the recreational game. Whether it is an old format restored or a novel one, the fact remains that cricket *qua* cricket does not fit snugly. Most cultural artifacts are like old soldiers. They do not die, they simply fade away, usually very slowly, for there are frequently adherents who mourn their passing and cling on to their remnants for as long as possible. Steam train addicts are an illustration. First-class county cricket may be approaching that degree of cultural limbo.

This is hardly a revelation. Rowland Bowen in his classic if controversial revisionist history of cricket writes of the sport's 'sudden and complete' decline, concluding 'It will continue, and in less than a hundred years, those who have enjoyed cricket will probably be a handful of dodderers; an episode in the social history of England, and to some extent of the world, will have closed.'[1] That was 1970 – and Rowland Bowen was canny enough to allow a hundred years for what Charles II might have termed 'an unconscionably long time a-dying'. There are still fifty-odd years to go – and Rowland Bowen had not been in a position to factor in the razor blades of Gillette, the tobacco of Benson and Hedges and the numerous insurance policies that came to cricket's aid by way of corporate sponsorship. Nor was he able to witness – he died in 1975 - the latest inventions and practices of ODI cricket. For all that, his prophecy in respect of English first-class cricket could well be on track.

Over the last year or so one has been able to take soundings, off the record, of several senior officials in the county game. Inevitably financial instability is the chief anxiety, with almost every first-class county in debt, albeit with some having adroitly structured that indebtedness, and, as is well-known, unable to sustain body and soul without central funding.

Television can be a fickle mistress. If the television companies decided that enough were enough because subscribers were declining in number (as seems, as of 2016, to be the case with football watchers) or advertisers were growing unhappy with the proceeds from their investments, matters could become critical. The game's sponsors, cheered to see their logos broadcast free of charge on the billboards around the grounds or even tattooed upon the very sacred turf and printed on the shirts and sweaters of the participants, would not be too pleased. An unpleasant fact is the near emptiness of venues around the world, especially for other than limited overs matches of note and interest. The TV cameras relish shots of the crowds, particularly when there are a dozen or so Elvis Presley *doppelgangers* or Richard Lionheart lookalikes to be spotted. That carnival element is much in demand.

Barren terraces cannot be hidden, which makes it look as if television is airing events which are dull and which no one wants to see. Imagine a TV show such as *Strictly Come Dancing* or *Britain's Got Talent* if there were a depleted studio audience. When this question has been raised, the answer urged is that televised cricket is inexpensive. You mount your cameras and other tackle for four or five days and you bounce nine or ten hours a day cricket and cricket talk off the satellite – and that's one whole channel taken care of. That, of course, is a simplified version of the argument but, certainly to the lay ear, it does sound somewhat over-confident.

Furthermore, and still on the fundamental subject of financial rectitude, what was suggested in conversation on one or two occasions, with a certain pressure of tongue in cheek but nonetheless with a clear-eyed realism, was that running a venue was fine and could be a decent business. What was economically disastrous was trying to manage a cricket team in that venue. Echoes of Thomas Lord; these arenas, several of them well-located and well-appointed, might be credible sites for all manner of activities, as several of them demonstrate, such as concerts, conferences, hospitality events and so forth. What wrecks the balance sheet is paying something like 500 cricketers to play before practically empty stands in all these stadia.

All this underlines the fragile nature of the construct. Unluckily for present ills, the English first-class tier was never organised on a sound economic basis. It was a tenet of that religio-imperial concept of its Victorian originators that a cricket should be protected from so sordid a taint as the commercial stain. It was emphatically not to be compared with the music hall or football or other elements of the thriving leisure industry of Victorian England. As we have noted, the coyness about amateurism or the disdain over paying Entertainments Tax subscribed to this disparagement of filthy lucre.

The Herculean task of transforming eighteen sacred temples into an economic proposition that attracts sufficient customers both to pay for itself at least in large part and fulfill its functions as the conduit to international stardom appears to be beyond the scale of human action.

It would be wrong to apportion blame. Even those who shuddered at the thought of cricket being soiled by overmuch stress on commercialisation have an appeal, in that they honestly believed in the purity and dignity of cricket. It is a view that seems quite attractive compared with money-grubbing. The old-time cricket professionals may thereby have been badly treated with condescension and occasionally contempt but we should be wary of making judgements solely by reference to modern standards.

By the standards of their times the working class pros were handled with reasonable thoughtfulness. Indeed, cricketing leaders like Lord Hawke, Lord Harris and, on his more grown-up days, W.G.Grace endeavoured to show a kindly respect to their paid colleagues. Equally, the low cost of entry for county and Test cricket enabled working class support to burgeon. It is true that higher prices may have led to lower revenue, as was the case at the London Artillery ground in the 18th century but there were no moves, as happened at Lord's in its early years, to deter the lower orders by a heightened entrance cost.

First-class county cricket fuelled the passion of true English cricket-lovers and still holds many of us in its alluring thrall. A Lancashire victory continues to give me an emotional, physically uplifting boost whereas an England win leaves me unmoved. (Such emotional, physically uplifting boosts have, unfortunately, been in fairly short supply as of late). Objectively, however, one has to accept the disappearance of an 'integrated culture', that substantial cross-class and also cross-generational factor that was the main building block of a compact society of relative social harmony.

Without that fundamental foundation and structure, the corresponding superstructure which included that cherished format of cricket cannot thrive. It may not perish but it cannot flourish. Precious little vanishes but much becomes a question of vestiges clinging on, at best never attaining the status of former times.

Although, with the collapse of the major manufacturing industries and similar economic factors, the relatively simple class system that appertained until the 1950s is now much complicated and variegated, one stark fact is clear. More so than in the previous epoch, there is a minority in what is certainly a more oligarchic society who command largish amounts of income and a majority on much sparser commons. It has been observed that both cricket players and watchers tend to fall into the former social band.

'O tempores o mores'; Cicero's famed terse phrase about other times having other customs is relevant. The ODI versions of cricket have been piecemeal, hurried and superficial essays in trying to adapt the game to a different social environment. They have failed conclusively in their

original intention of acting as a route-way to watching first-class cricket. They may even have run the risk of throwing out the baby with the bathwater. Moreover, the length of these tourneys has been reduced to a minimum of twenty overs. The initial limited overs version was 65 overs, then described as the minimal amount for a 'proper' game of cricket. As support for 60, 50 and 40 overs matches languished a little, Twenty20 fixtures – currently described, inevitably, as the lowest over rate possible for reasonable cricket – are now all the rage. Probably the safest prediction one might hazard about the future of cricket is that, as the Twenty20 furore subsides, a ten over competition will be on offer, bringing cricket ever more nearly to parity with the football codes in respect of the duration of the game. Reduced teams and even single-wicket gladiatorial contests are further possibilities.[2]

In addressing these issues some years ago, I reached very much the same conclusions and, ever conscious of the need to economise on one's material, I find that a repetition of those thoughts has stood the test of time and serve adequately for a final commentary.[3]

'Cricket's best chances lie in another swing in society's pendulum, back to a situation of social coherence and cultural togetherness. First-class cricket, as a spectator sport, might thrive again. It would be a dreadful calamity if, in our endeavours to save cricket for the consumerist, self-centred generations, we actually maimed it beyond repair and were left with nothing of cricketing value when times become more propitious. In the meantime, Erasmus taught us that we 'plough the sands in vain'. At present the soil of our country is unfavourable for the cultivation of first-class cricket; both soil and plant require our urgent and profound treatment.'

During the spring of 2017, the England and Wales Cricket Board announced proposals from 2020 onwards for a new Twenty20 competition with eight franchised teams, playing games during the cricketing high-season of July and August, and the drier months when traditionally the English twirlers have come into their own. The announcement followed a winter when the national side suffered defeats in spin-friendly conditions in Bangladesh and India, but fear not, as the ever ailing counties will be compensated with £1.3m each for their troubles in agreeing to the new proposals which is set to see many of the four-day Championship matches being shoehorned into the chronological fringes of spring and early autumn. It was a final – for now – piece of evidence for the case made in these pages about the gradual diminution of first-class county cricket.

---

1.   Bowen op.cit pp 256/257.
2.   Perhaps prophetically the TV series *Midsomer Murders* on 16 January 2017 entitled *'Last Man out'*, featured a globally franchised ten overs' competition. Its Australian entrepreneur was the murder victim
3.   Eric Midwinter *Cricket Lore 'Putting the Squeeze on Cricket; part one Cricket and the Integrated Culture* vol 5 issue 2 and *'Putting the Squeeze on Cricket; part two Cricket and the Hourglass Society'* vol 5 issue 3 (2002/05).

Acknowledgements

As a member and former senior officer of the ACS I am both gratified by and grateful for the opportunity afforded me of contributing to the association's new Cricket Witness series. Having watched cricket since a child, played a little, read a lot, talked even more and then written about cricket for well nigh 40 years, one would need a lengthy roster to pay tribute to all who have contributed to an historical text prepared by such an octogenarian cricket-lover. There are, however, more immediate dues of appreciation to be paid, namely, to John Winnifrith for his meticulous proof-reading and comments, Andrew Hignell for his generous and positive encouragement and advice at the origins and throughout the writing of this book and to David Jeater for his meticulous editing of the draft typescript. In particular, I wish to thank Andrew for his perceptive researches that led to both the cover design and the central display of photographs. These add very effectively and relevantly to the tenor of this study. I stand indebted to these three fine stalwarts of cricket scholarship.

Index